COOKERY
OF THE
PRAIRIE HOMESTEADER

by
LOUISE K. NICKEY

Illustrations by David Jersey

THE TOUCHSTONE PRESS
P. O. Box 81
Beaverton, Oregon 97005

I dedicate this book
COOKERY OF THE PRAIRIE HOMESTEADER
in loving memory of Grandpa and Mamma
and
to my husband John Malcolm Nickey
who so faithfully sampled all the foods
I "kitchen tested" and encouraged me during
all the months I have worked on this project.

CONTENTS

PREFACE

I was born in southern Indiana and at the age of five went with my family to homestead in eastern Montana. I lived on the prairies until I was 16 years old.

Mamma then moved to Bozeman, Montana, so my sister and I could finish high school and attend Montana State College. After receiving my degree I taught commercial subjects, drama and speech until I married John M. Nickey, a former grade school friend, in 1938.

We have two children, John Jr. and Pearl Louise, and four grand-children — Stephanie and Michael, Johnny and Wendy.

After John and Pearl were in the 5th and 6th grades I returned to teaching, but this time in the field of English and continued with drama and speech.

I received my master's degree in 1962 in English and education.

I taught intermittently until my retirement in 1969. I always enjoyed teaching and one of my treasured memories was the receiving of the plaque for "Coach of the Year" for Montana in speech and debate for the school year of 1968-69.

A little over two years ago I began the "kitchen testing" for recipe accuracy of the good foods that Mamma used to cook for us.

Until Mamma was past 90 she was still baking her one-crust apple pie which was considered the pie of perfection by her friends and relatives.

For several years my daughter Pearl Louise has wanted me to write the story of homestead life on the prairies. So finally I have combined information regarding the preparation of our foods with incidents of our life, as I remember them, in "Cookery of the Prairie Homesteader."

This book deals somewhat with the men and women who built homes and towns and schools from the prairie lands. They turned the sod, fenced their claims, survived droughts, blizzards, hail storms, tornado-like winds, and prairie fires.

Mamma was the staying force in my sister Olive's and my life. She kept house and cooked the meals, kept us neat and clean, doctored us when we were sick, and always insisted on truthfulness and good man-ners. As both mother and teacher she was a martinet in seeing that we mastered the three "R's" — reading, writing and arithmetic, plus grammar, geography, history and spelling.

Mamma's foods were well-cooked and well-seasoned. Her style was inherited from a line of good cooks and based on recipes from the English, the German and the French, with a distinct flavor of the deep south. Olive and I learned to do simple cooking at an early age.

Son John spent several years in the Air Force in North Carolina and after a celebration dinner on his return to Montana, he remarked, "Now I know why I like southern cooking. I have eaten it all my life."

I have kitchen tested all these recipes and think my husband, and son and daughter and their families have been very considerate in taste-testing and eating my foods. For example, one day I made five batches of ginger cookies and another day I served three kinds of potatoes for dinner.

I do hope you, the reader, will enjoy these stories of homestead days, and that you will cook these basic foods and find them as delicious as Olive and I did when Mamma cooked them for us when we were little.

L. K. N.

Bozeman, Montana
1976

The families moved onto these quarter sections in March of 1907. The homesteads were taken in the fall of 1906.

The town of Flandrem was nine and a half miles Southwest. Culbertson was thirty-five miles to the south, and was at the end of the Great Northern track.

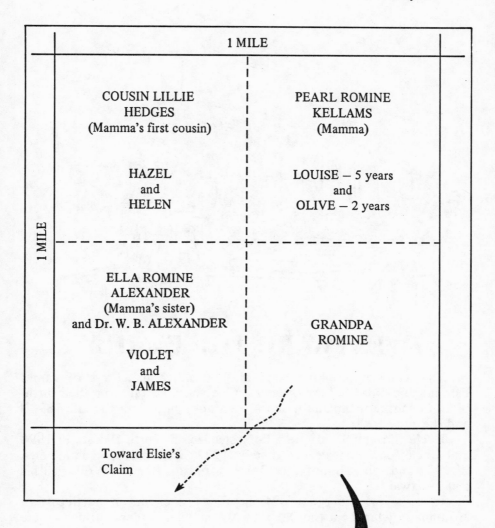

1 MILE

1 MILE

COUSIN LILLIE
HEDGES
(Mamma's first cousin)

HAZEL
and
HELEN

PEARL ROMINE
KELLAMS
(Mamma)

LOUISE — 5 years
and
OLIVE — 2 years

ELLA ROMINE
ALEXANDER
(Mamma's sister)
and Dr. W. B. ALEXANDER

VIOLET
and
JAMES

GRANDPA
ROMINE

Toward Elsie's
Claim

Culbertson

MONTANA

WESTWARD THE FAMILY

The tall, goodlooking sons and attractive daughters of James Romine and Olive Sidney Stites Romine ventured far from their birthplace in southern Indiana near the Kentucky border in the late 1890's and the early 1900's.

Uncle Sid and Uncle Bert homesteaded in North Dakota in 1898 and Uncle John homesteaded there in 1902. Grandmother Romine died in 1904 and soon Grandfather Romine sold his farm and followed his sons westward.

In 1906, at the age of 74, he filed on claims in north-eastern Montana not far from the Dakota and Canadian borders during the late fall, for himself, his two daughters and a niece.

In the spring of 1907 the remainder of the family came to Montana, by emigrant train and arrived in Culbertson which was the end of the line. Railroads encouraged the settlement of the west by offering low rates on day coaches to homesteaders. I still remember that coach — the prickly green plush seats, the uncarpeted floors, the coal burning stove, the small, cramped lavatory and the taste of the brackish drinking water.

The box car with household furniture, livestock and the framework for the barn which had been cut from oak trees on Grandfather's Indiana farm was already there. Uncle Bert and Jim Hevron, a cousin, had come with the box car and were met by Grandpa in Culbertson. They had set up a big tent, and had a stove, cooking utensils and beds.

We lived in the tent for nearly two weeks waiting for the snow to melt enough so the stage could leave. The women and children slept in the hotel and the men slept in the tent.

The first morning in Culbertson I was both excited and frightened. A big Indian came to the small campfire near the tent. He had long, heavy plaits hanging forward over his shoulders. He told my grandfather in sign language that he wanted to buy a horse we called Joe. The Indian held up his hand opening and closing it until he had counted twenty-five indicating he would give $25 for it. He didn't get the horse, and Joe, a family pet, lived and grew old on the prairies.

We became accustomed, in those two weeks of waiting, to look up and perhaps see some Indian man, woman, or child standing by the flap of the tent watching the grown-ups at work and the children at play.

Finally we left on the stage for the homestead. The stage was a light weight uncovered wagon with two seats. It was March, and March in Montana may be cold and windy, with rain and sleet and snow. We were covered well with blankets and did not get cold as the horses walked and trotted over muddy roads and through the remains of snow drifts.

It was a long 35 miles from Culbertson, by stage through the lonesome land, with lay-overs at the shacks of still earlier homesteaders, to Grandpa's shack where cold winds blew through windows covered only by gunny sacks.

"Horse trading"

It was here in the prairie shack that my sister Olive and my little cousin Lelia had the red measles. There were anxious days while the small girls were ill, and happy relief when the fever went down and they began to improve.

That was a busy summer for the settlers in the new land. Grandpa's house was finished. Doors and windows replaced the gunny sacks. A coal house, hall and pantry was built on the back of the house. The big barn was put up, a landmark in the country for many years and it still stands, lonesomely, surrounded by great wheat fields. The homes of the other members of the family were built, plowing was done, crops were planted and gardens started.

Most of my memories of homestead days on the prairies are happy memories. Of course there were thunder storms, hailstorms, prairie fires, droughts, blizzards. But the happiness stays with me — memories of warming weather and the greening of the grass as spring advanced, gentle breezes as we ran through the heavy grasses, flaky clouds scurrying across the wide blue skies, the heat of the long days which merged into Indian summer, the coming of fall and winter, coasting down huge snowdrifts, the excitement of butchering and making sausage and lard, playing in the house by the cozy warmth of the stove while a blizzard raged outside. There are memories of Christmas, Fourth of July, Thanksgiving, box suppers, school days, taffy pulls, threshing time and cousins visiting from Canada, North Dakota and Indiana.

Mamma read to us and cooked for us. We had good food, and always plenty, and as far as I know so did our neighbors. When we went visiting or had guests, feasts were common.

When I read stories today about homesteaders starving it seems unreal. Of course the women of the family came west as traditionally fine cooks and they maintained that tradition. They had to adjust to the cookery of new foods, as well as continue with their heritage. The results were delicious and nourishing.

From these memories comes my book *Cookery of the Prairie Homesteader.* I have used the foods we ate and have "kitchen tested" all recipes for accurate proportions. Mamma, like most cooks of that era, did little measuring of ingredients — it might be 2 or 2½ cups of flour, about a cup of sugar, a dash of salt, a pinch of soda, two or three eggs, and butter the size of a walnut.

I have made suggestions for the use of the recipes in menus that make nutritious and well-balanced meals. In that day, as I recall, our meals were surprisingly well-balanced. Grandpa did the gardening and since he had the "proverbial green thumb" we had all the usual garden produce. Grandpa stored many of these vegetables in the cellar for use as fresh foods during the long, cold winters. Some of the foods were processed as pickles, and some were dried. A big jar of sauerkraut was made.

As homesteaders we gathered the wild fruits of the plains — wild plums, buffalo or bison berries, chokecherries, sandcherries, and June berries or service berries. We also found new methods of using the standard foods available to us in order to give more variety to our diet.

The families raised and butchered animals for beef and pork and dried beef, and made sausage, ham and bacon. We raised chickens for both meat and eggs. We had cows, so we also had milk, butter, cream and cottage cheese. Prairie chickens and sage hens were plentiful. There were fish in the Little Muddy, and Big Muddy (Missouri) and Medicine Lake. We stored 600 to 800 pounds of sugar and flour each fall and ordered a big supply of groceries from the Sears Roebuck Grocery Department in Chicago.

Much of the food was traditionally American but some was Scandinavian as many Danes and Norwegians settled in the northeastern section of Montana.

My book deals with the preparation of the many foods we ate, seasoned with factual anecdotes, and blended with memories of some of the phenomena of nature on the prairie lands in the early 1900's.

CHEWY GINGER COOKIES

My cousins, James and Violet, my sister, Olive, and I particularly liked ginger cookies. In looking over some old recipes the other day I noticed that Mamma had a notation on the ginger cookie card: "James likes these."

I well remember one spring day when Mamma made ginger cookies. Violet had come to visit Olive and me for a couple of hours and we were playing hide-and-seek at the barn and granary.

The granary was two large rooms attached to the back of the barn, lean-to fashion. I was "it" when Violet and Olive just disappeared. I simply could not find them. I searched in the barn, the henhouse, behind the feed grinder, and even peeped in the closet. I felt that they were some place in the granary, but those big dark rooms were fearsome when I was by myself. I called and called "Olly-olly-oxen free," but they neither answered or came. Finally I latched both the granary doors and went to the house feeling very disgruntled.

Mamma was just taking a pan of ginger cookies from the oven, and of course she asked, "Where are the girls?" and I answered very truthfully, "I think they are in the granary," omitting to tell her that I had latched the doors. She gave me two cookies and two apiece for Olive and Violet. When I returned to the granary, I knew quite well where the girls were. They were demanding loudly and none too politely to be let out. I began to enjoy myself. I ate my cookies while they watched through a crack in the door, and then to make matters worse I slowly ate their share, "ohing" and "ahing" about how delicious they were. They continued to bang on the door while calling me mean names.

They banged so hard on the door that I was afraid the latch wouldn't hold so I ran to the house, and sat down by the table to read an Elsie Dinsmore book. The kitchen was hot from the spring sunshine on the sloping roof and the heat of the coal cooking stove. Mamma told me to peel some potatoes, but even that was better than returning to the granary.

When Violet and Olive finally came in their faces were red, but they said nothing about the granary doors. I really didn't think they would as we had a very definite code in regard to tattletales. We had some cookies and milk, but I didn't go out to play anymore, as I just felt more comfortable in the house.

This is Mamma's recipe for ginger cookies. **Cream 1 cup of sugar and 1 cup of butter.** Add **1 cup of sorghum** and mix thoroughly. (Other molasses may be used but I think sorghum gives the best flavor.) To this add **1 teaspoon soda, 2 teaspoons of ginger, and 2½ cups of unsifted flour.** Mix all of this together until it makes a smooth dough and divide into fourths for easy working. The dough will handle better if it is refrigerated for 2 or 3 hours. Lightly flour the board and rolling pin and roll the dough to a thickness of about ¼-inch.

When you first begin mixing the ingredients set the oven for 375 degrees to preheat the oven.

I use a 2½ inch cookie cutter and gently lift the rich tender cookies onto a greased and floured cookie sheet with a pancake turner. Place the pan in the preheated oven and bake for 10 to 12 minutes — checking carefully as the cookies will scorch very easily. When they are a very pale brown they are done. At once remove from the cookie sheet with a pancake turner and place on a folded cloth to cool. The cloth prevents the cookie from becoming too dry. A cooling rack would also make ridges in the tender cookie as it is very soft when it comes from the oven.

Save all scraps as you cut out the cookies and after all the dough has been rolled and cut, work the scraps into a ball and roll out for another baking.

With a 2½ inch cutter, this recipe makes about 3½ dozen cookies. If you are baking for a special occasion be sure that none of the children or men folks are around or you won't have enough for your plans. If you are baking just for family use, call them to the kitchen for those piping hot chewy cookies that may be dunked in cold milk or fresh coffee and enjoy a tasty snack.

When the grandchildren visit, stir up some ginger cookie dough and get out the various shaped cookie cutters. Michael especially enjoys using the gingerbread man cutter. Roll the dough thicker than the regular cookies and hand over the cutter to a Stephanie, a Michael or a Johnny. Use a wide pancake turner to lift the cutouts to the cookie sheet, and have raisins and currants so each child may decorate his own ginger cookie man.

If you have the patience, allow them to cut several ginger cookie men and when they are baked, call in the small fry of the neighborhood for a party.

A good time and a noisy time will be had by all, and the mothers will love you!

By the way, the girls finally told me that they had climbed up on top of the eight foot divider between the two granaries and sat there in the dimness of the windowless building. The latch had not given way with their pounding on the door. Violet had found the end of a wire sticking out from the wall and had broken off a piece by bending it back and forth. She poked this through the door crack and lifted the latch. She always was clever.

SPRING COMES TO THE PRAIRIES

Sharp bitter winds of March faded into warm breezes and gentle rains. Grasses suddenly greened, life throbbed throughout the prairie. Meadow larks sang, frogs croaked, small cottontails, their long ears flopping, hopped through the grasses. Geese honked on high as they flew northward.

COUSIN ELSIE

Elsie is the daughter of Uncle Ben Romine, Grandpa's oldest son who had died of typhoid years before.

Elsie came to Montana in 1908 to teach school and filed on a homestead about a mile southwest of Grandpa's homestead in 1910.

She would teach in Montana each summer and when winter came would return to Indiana to teach there.

Olive and I were always very excited when she came back in the spring. Elsie was a wonderful big cousin, and we loved her. We could hardly wait until she opened her trunk for we wanted to see all her new clothes. I will never forget one beautiful waist. It was a green plaid taffeta and I thought nothing could be prettier.

Elsie boarded or batched near her school during the week, helped Mamma with cleaning, baking, washing, ironing, hauling water, on Saturday. Then on Saturday evening Olive and I took turns walking over to her shack with her in the early dusk of the evening with the last rays of the sun slanting across the prairies. I loved those walks. The evening breezes blew against us. Birds cheeped in the grass and sometimes startled us by flying up almost in our faces.

We came to the shack and soon the soft yellow glow of the coal oil lamp lighted the small room. Elsie let the bed down from behind its sheet curtain on the wall. I liked sleeping there, just Elsie and I by ourselves on the prairie.

CHERRY PRESERVES

Breakfast was a treat, when we had cherry preserves made by Aunt Gertie, Elsie's mother, from southern Indiana fruit. Aunt Gertie used May cherries for her preserves.

The cherries were pitted and for **each cup of pitted cherries** she added **3/4 cup of sugar and 1/4 cup of water.** The fruit and sugar simmered slowly on the back of the stove until a thick syrup formed. This was cherry preserves and was put into jelly glasses.

EASTER EGGS

It was a very wet dark and dreary day, that Saturday before Easter so many years ago on the prairies. To make matters worse Good Friday had been a beautiful day with floods of sunshine, the birds singing vigorously, the gophers cheeping and flipping their tails as they popped in and out of their holes. We weren't really able to enjoy that sunshine because we had to sit in the school room and do our lessons.

Now we had this dismal day, and couldn't go out to play. It was so rainy Mamma hadn't even washed clothes. Olive and I had practically dented the glass in the window as we stood so long pressing our foreheads against the cold window panes, trying to see through that gray drizzle.

We begged to go outside and play anyway, but that idea was soon squelched. Finally Mamma said that she would hardboil some eggs and we could help her dye them for Easter Sunday.

Our unhappiness left immediately, and our warm kitchen seemed a cheery place to be.

Mamma picked out **2 dozen white eggs,** put them in a large kettle of cold water, slowly brought them to a gentle boil and cooked them for 20 minutes. She put a soft folded towel on the bottom of the kettle to keep the eggs from breaking.

While the eggs were cooking, Mamma found **6 old cups,** dropped **a tablet of Easter egg dye** in each cup and filled each one **3/4ths full of hot water.** Olive and I used old spoons and mixed and stirred the dyes. We then added **2 teaspoons vinegar** to each cup.

Mamma helped us lift the eggs from the kettle into the dyes. We colored eggs red, green, yellow, orange, blue and purple. We also cut out designs from a sheet of paper in the Easter egg dye package — birds, flowers, and butterflies. These cutouts we placed on the dyed eggs then covered the picture with a cloth soaked in vinegar. When we removed the cloth from the paper the picture was transferred to the egg. We thought they were beautiful — although the eggs were sometimes quite splotchy and the pictures crooked. This was our first time dyeing eggs — as the "Easter Rabbit" had always done it before.

Mamma put the eggs in a big bowl in the center of the kitchen table.

We were so engrossed with admiring the eggs that we had not noticed that the gray drizzle had lightened and a shaft of sunlight flowed through the west window across the eggs, increasing their brightness and beauty.

The eggs were forgotten as we raced to put on our overshoes, coats, and caps and dashed out into that clear bright afternoon. The dazzling sunlight, the clear blue sky, the greening grass, the birds singing made a new day.

That night our beautiful Easter eggs were hidden, and we had an Easter egg hunt Sunday morning. We kept some of the prettiest ones, shelled the remainder and Mamma made deviled eggs for dinner.

DEVILED EGGS

Deviled eggs are easy to make and are always good for lunches, picnics, dinners, and parties.

Place **6 eggs** (at least 4 or 5 days old) in a pan, cover with cold water and bring slowly to a boil. Older eggs shell better. Boil twenty minutes. Pour off the hot water and immediately pour very cold water over the eggs. Drain off and add more cold water, let stand 5 minutes. Tap the egg on each end and the sides breaking the shell then lightly roll the egg 3 or 4 times on a hard surface with the palm of the hand. In most cases these eggs will now shell or peel very nicely.

After the eggs are shelled, cut them in half, either lengthwise or crosswise, and remove the yolks. Mash the yolks, **add 2 tablespoons butter or cream, ¼ teaspoon pepper, ¼ teaspoon salt, 2 tablespoons sugar, and 1 tablespoon vinegar.** Mix until creamy, refill the hollowed out whites of the egg.

There are several ways to give interesting variety to deviled eggs.

1. **Add 2 rounding tablespoons chow-chow** to the already seasoned egg yolk and mix well.

2. **Add 1 tablespoon minced onion and 1 tablespoon shredded pimiento** to the egg yolks.

3. **Mix bits of those small Norwegian sardines** with the yolks and pile into the hard boiled whites.

4. Spoon the creamed and seasoned egg yolks into the hollowed whites. Top the egg with a **slice of stuffed olive.**

For breakfast on Easter we had soft boiled eggs, hot biscuits and jelly, a dish of applesauce and milk. Grandpa had coffee.

SOFT-BOILED EGGS

Mamma soft-boiled several eggs. I like my soft-boiled egg cooked five minutes. That is, five minutes from the time the egg begins to boil. The white is firm, and the yellow is soft, but not raw and runny.

The three minute egg is practically raw.

On Easter Sunday morning, each person was allowed to eat as many eggs as he could. Olive and I only managed 3 or 4 apiece. The white was firm; the yellow soft but not as runny as the uncooked yolk. Grandpa ate 6 to 8 of these soft-boiled eggs. He took a sharp knife, brought the blade-edge down on the side of the egg and clipped through the shell just to the egg yolk, which did not break. He then scooped the egg from the half shells into a serving dish. He seasoned his eggs with butter, salt and pepper.

I found it very difficult to open my soft-boiled eggs without breaking the yellow and having it smeared over the dish, the egg shell and my fingers.

SCRAMBLED EGGS

I like old-fashioned scrambled eggs. Heat a 12-inch iron skillet to medium heat. While the skillet is heating, break the eggs, one at a time into a small bowl, then pour into a mixing bowl, until you have the required number of eggs. Place **4 tablespoons butter or bacon grease** into the heated skillet. Pour the eggs into the melted shortening and when the whites begin to thicken stir the eggs gently with a large spoon. Cook for a minute, and stir again. The eggs become firm and the whites and yolks are cooked in definite white and yellow marbleized streaks.

Serve with crisp bacon, buttermilk biscuits, choke-cherry jelly, and a dish of stewed, dried raspberries.

FRIED EGGS

Fried eggs were a popular food in homestead days as well as now. Most of the homesteaders had a flock of chickens — which provided both meat and eggs.

We had fresh eggs nearly all year. In late fall, Mamma packed several dozen eggs in boxes of oats, or salt. The oats or salt kept air from the eggs and they were usable for many weeks until the hens began laying in the spring.

Grandpa, Mamma and I liked our eggs fried in a **small amount of bacon fryings or butter.** Break the eggs, one at a time, pour into the medium hot shortening, spacing the eggs so they just barely touch. Gently turn the egg over being careful not to break the yellow. Cook another minute then serve.

Olive liked her egg well done, so Mamma cooked hers another 2 or 3 minutes.

For soft-fried eggs I cover the frying pan with a tight lid. The steam cooks the tops of the eggs and it is not necessary to turn the egg over. Salt and pepper when the white of the egg is firm (the yellow is soft), then serve. Top a hot buttered piece of toast with a steamed egg, serve with a generous slice of ham, some more toast and buffalo berry jelly. A dish of prunes and cocoa or coffee goes well with this breakfast.

POACHED EGGS

When Olive and I were little girls, Mamma would poach eggs for us if we had an upset stomach. She poached the egg in hot water. Heat 1½ to 2 inches of water just to the boiling point in a heavy skillet, turn the heat to low and slide the egg from a small dish into the water. The water must *not* be boiling because the egg white will scatter and be broken. The water must be hot enough to set or coagulate the white so the eggs make a small mound in the water.

I like the white well done. If you put the bread in the toaster just after you slip the eggs into the water, they usually are cooked enough by the time the toast is well browned and buttered. Either toast or crackers with poached egg works for upsets.

Try well crisped salt pork with poached egg on toast, apple butter, and a dish of stewed dried peaches sometime for breakfast.

The salt pork should be parboiled and set aside to drain the evening before. When you start breakfast, heat a large skillet to medium, add 1 tablespoon lard, dip the salt pork in flour and begin frying. While the salt pork is cooking, set the table, start the coffee, slice the bread for toast, and put the water on to heat for the eggs. The salt pork is best cooked rather slowly so it will brown, not burn and be well done.

HELPFUL HINTS ON HANDLING EGGS

— Hold raw eggs under warm running water for about ½ minute. When the egg is broken, the white pulls away from the shell more easily.

— Recipes sometimes call for just the whites or just the yolks of the egg. Get two containers — one for the yellows and one for the whites. Break the egg by tapping the side of the egg on the edge of a dish or the table.

Hold the egg over the bowl. Pull the egg open where cracked, and allow the white to run into the bowl, keeping the yellow in ½ of the shell. One part of the shell is now empty. Pour the yellow into the empty half allowing any remaining white to go into the bowl. The white and yolk should now be separated. If not return the yolk back to the first half shell.

Be careful as you shift the yolk back and forth that it does not break, since even a drop or two of yellow in the white keeps it from whipping into satisfactory stiff white peaks.

I have found a little gadget at a novelty store — an egg separator. It is much like a deeply cupped tablespoon with slots on the sides. The cup holds the yolk, and the white slides through the slot. I put the "egg separator" on the top of a glass, so I do not have to hold it, and can more easily break the egg for separating.

The egg white is poured into the bowl for beating. The yolks are added to a basic salad recipe.

— Break just one egg into a small container, inspect, then empty in mixing bowl or cooking pan. Some eggs may have brown spots or bloody spots. Only occasionally is blood found in an egg purchased from a grocery store, as the law requires the eggs to be candled.

An egg is candled by placing it over a strong light, and then looking through the egg shell to see if there are any spots. I have been told these bloody egg whites are all right to use, but I just don't like to see a bloody egg.

If you have your own chickens and use your own eggs without candling — it is not unusual to find some blood discoloration or other defects in the egg whites.

— When beating egg whites, check carefully to be sure the bowl and beaters are clean, dry and have absolutely no grease. Any sign of shortening will keep the eggs from beating up well. A pinch of salt added when you begin to beat the eggs seems to help the egg whites beat into peaks. One eighth teaspoon of cream of tartar promotes the greater expansion of the egg white.

— Eggs beat much better at room temperature, so remove the required number of eggs from the refrigerator perhaps an hour in advance.

— A sickroom dish was a poached egg, a teaspoon of butter, a sprinkle of salt and pepper, 2 or 3 tablespoons of water in which the egg was poached. Chop up the egg and mix with the ingredients. Crumble in a cracker. This tastes good, and slides down easily, if your throat is sore.

MUSHROOMS

Mushrooms were not a luxury item to the homesteaders and their prairie children. Spring usually came early on the plains and hot sunny days would be interrupted by quick spring showers. A sudden night shower would leave the soil damp and pulsing with growing things. The grass would suddenly seem greener, the strong smell of the earth would rise in the humid air. Mamma would say "Girls, see if you can find some mushrooms," and mostly we could.

There would be small round humps poking through the warm soil between green plants. We would run barefooted over the weeds and grasses softened by rain, but watching for small pin cushion cacti and the buttercups, and picking small violets and bluebells.

Many times we would find enough mushrooms to fill a quart bucket, not far from the house. The round curved tops and pink undersides of these delicacies would be carefully washed then simmered until done, for either dinner or for supper. They would be seasoned with butter, salt and pepper to taste. Rich milk and a thickener would be

added. Mamma filled a big square China bowl with the creamed mushrooms and made a big plate of buttered toast and we had all we could
eat.

Mamma sometimes slowly cooked the mushrooms in a skillet in two
or three tablespoons of butter until done. These were good, but I really
preferred the mushrooms with milk over toast.

Gradually the mushrooms almost disappeared as more and more of
the prairies were plowed and crops planted. We nearly always found a
few though if we went down the lane and out into the big pasture, after
one of those warm spring rains.

— Many mushrooms are poisonous, so we were very careful in the
variety we picked.

The edible ones we found on the prairie are known as the field or
meadow mushroom. They usually grow from 2 to 4 inches tall and have
a fleshy top 1¼ to 4 inches across. The top is slightly cupped and the
meaty part is white, with pink gills. In the new mushroom the gills are

covered by a membrane that stretches from the stem to the edge of the cap. As the mushroom grows the membrane pulls away from the stem showing the soft pink. The mushroom grows very rapidly and in just a few hours reaches maturity.

Mamma told Olive and me to pull a piece of the skin from the top of the mushroom. If the flesh underneath had a rough dull texture, it was edible. If it was smooth and shiny, the mushroom was poisonous. We always checked carefully and Mamma rechecked.

Never pick your own mushrooms unless you have an authority to help you.

I emphasize that some mushrooms are poisonous and very dangerous.

THICKENER

I use what I call a thickener to make gravies from broth and sauces for creamed dishes.

Use a ½ **pint** or **pint fruit jar.** Pour into the jar ½ **cup water** and **6 tablespoons flour,** stir well, then cover and shake hard several times, until the flour and water look like a thick smooth cream.

This thickener, when used with **2 cups of rich broth** or **clear meat** or **chicken soup,** makes 2½ cups of gravy. Pour the thickener into the simmering liquid, just a little at a time, stirring constantly until you have the desired consistency.

AUNT HATTIE'S FRIED FROGS LEGS

For two years Uncle Bert and Aunt Hattie lived in a house a quarter of a mile north of Grandpa's house and barn. This house was on Mamma's homestead. Uncle Sid and Aunt Emma often came down from Canada to visit. Uncle Bert and Uncle Sid would then go coyote hunting. They would take their two wolf hounds, a great Russian gray-hound and a shaggy long haired mutt called Joe. I think they really liked Joe the best. He couldn't run as fast as the other dogs, but he was a scrapper and they liked to tell the story of Joe going into a hole after a coyote, and bringing him out. Joe was badly cut up and didn't do any more hunting for a few weeks. They rode horseback all over the low hills and flats on the east side of the Little Muddy hunting coyotes — and pushing back range cattle from the crops on the homesteads. Our fields had not yet been fenced.

The flats had many sloughs and marshy places and here Uncle Bert found big jumping frogs. He kept talking about fried frog legs until Aunt Hattie gave in and consented to fry them for him if he caught enough for a mess.

We were all invited to supper the evening that Aunt Hattie fried the frog legs. I was quite dubious about those frog legs as Uncle Bert told Olive and me that the legs would keep jumping and might jump out of the pan. As I remember they didn't jump and they tasted much like fried chicken.

The frog legs are skinned, seasoned with salt, rolled in flour, or dipped in egg and cracker crumbs, and fried in deep fat.

As we walked home after supper, the skies were colored by the Northern Lights — reds and purples, oranges, yellows and greens. The light seemed to reach away above our heads and then sway back and forth as if they were great ribbons waving in a high wind. Olive and I stood very near to Mamma and Elsie, awed by the great masses of color in the northern skies.

BUTTER, BUTTERMILK AND COTTAGE CHEESE

Mamma made her own butter and cottage cheese. She churned about once a week. The cream was saved from the morning milkings each day. Milk was poured through a sterilized cloth and strainer into heavy stone crocks. Each morning Mamma would spoon the heavy cream that had risen to the top of the milk into a big jar to sour. Some of the sweet cream might be saved for cooking or to use on desserts or in coffee.

The skimmed milk, which was still quite rich was used for drinking and cooking, and that not used by the family was given to the cats, dogs, chickens and pigs. Some of the skimmed milk was allowed to clabber.

COTTAGE CHEESE

Clabber milk is milk that has become sour and is thick with a texture much like a perfect custard. I like to take a spoon and eat this quivery clabber milk if it has barely turned sour.

Mamma poured the clabbered milk into a large kettle, and put it on the back of the stove where the heat was very low.

Gradually the clabber, as it slowly warmed, would begin to separate into chunks and the whey would form. It might take two hours or maybe longer for the cheese chunks or curds and whey to separate. When separated, Mamma poured the curds in to a cloth bag, or strainer, or a colander and allowed to stand and drain until all the whey was gone. The solid that was left was clabber cheese, cottage cheese, or "smearcase," which was a colloquial expression used in our neighborhood in Indiana.

If you make cottage cheese you will be more successful if you use the raw milk. Also be very careful not to overheat the clabber, as the cheese chunks will become hard. If a few drops dropped on the wrist feels very warm, that temperature is all right for the temperature of the clabber milk.

Sometimes the slightly heated clabber cheese was put in a cloth bag and fastened to the clothes line, where it drained in the sun and the wind.

Mamma took the drained cheese, poured sweet cream over it and stirred until the cheese was thoroughly moistened. She then added salt and sometimes black pepper. We would have a big bowl of very excellent "smearcase" for dinner or supper.

Grandpa had a hired man, who did like food, but in unusual ways. He stacked his potatoes on top of his meat, added vegetables, and if there was "smearcase" used a generous helping of it on top of his vegetables, then poured syrup over the whole thing.

BUTTER MAKING

Butter making day usually found me at the dasher of the churn. We had a tall stone churn with a wooden lid, and a wooden dasher. The dasher was made by two thick crossed boards with a long wooden handle fastened in the center of the boards. The handle was much like a broom handle and went through a hole in the lid.

The dasher was scalded with hot water and rubbed with salt and put into the churn which might be half full of sour cream, then the lid was put on. The salt on the dasher helped prevent the fat sticking to it. My job was to work that dasher up and down, up and down, until butter came! Sometimes I thought it took hours.

If the day was hot it might be hard to get the butter to form. At first the cream became almost like a thick whipped cream, then grad-

ually it began to separate into lumpy small yellow particles, and the buttermilk came. The butter might not gather if the day and the cream were too warm. We watched the handle of the dasher just above the lid to see the small particles of yellow butter form. We added a cup of cold water and kept on working the dasher slowly. Gradually the butter gathered into a big lump.

If the cream and the day was chilly, it was sometimes difficult to make butter, too. Then we might have to add quite warm water a half cup at a time in order to make the cream break and the butter come. The cold cream made a better butter, but was harder to churn.

Homemade buttermilk is a very good and refreshing drink, and we had a glass of buttermilk as soon as the butter was removed from the churn.

The butter was turned out into a large stone crock and as much milk as possible pressed out with a wooden butter paddle. Mamma always scalded the paddle and rubbed it with salt.

In working out any liquid from the butter, take just a small amount at a time and press it against the side of the crock with the paddle. As the liquid collects in the crock pour it out, and repeat until all the butter has been worked a little at a time. If the butter is soft, pour on cold water and allow to stand for half an hour. It is much easier to work if it is firmer. It may be necessary to wash the butter 3 or 4 times to remove all the buttermilk. The water should be clear before you stop washing the butter.

Just before packing the butter in the mold, Mamma would put in some salt and work it into the butter, then she would taste it. Olive and I were right there to get a taste. Maybe it would be just right, or she might have to add more salt. Very few things taste better than fresh sweet butter!

Mamma packed the butter in a pound wooden butter mold. The mold was oblong and had a flower design carved in the inside top. When filled, the mold was opened, and there was a beautiful oblong pound of butter with a flower on top. A dampened white cloth covered the butter which was stored for future use. In hot weather, Mamma covered the butter with clean white cloths and stored it with salt packed around it.

Mamma seldom sold butter, as she only milked one or two cows, and the family used most of it. Occasionally, if we had extra, she sold some.

BUTTERMILK BISCUITS

I was making buttermilk biscuits when I was seven years old. Picture a small serious girl standing on a small green box by the kitchen table, with her hands in a pan of flour. She wore a dark wool dress, with long sleeves and a high neck, that was practically covered by a full length blue checked apron that also had long sleeves. She wore black ribbed stockings and black button shoes. Two big ribbon bows tied her plaited and rolled hair behind each ear.

The kitchen was warm and cozy on those cold winter days, when temperatures sometimes would dip to 60 degrees below zero. The old-fashioned coal stove radiated quivering heat that pushed back the cold. The teakettle hummed and sang. A wall coal oil lamp dimly lighted the room with a yellow glow.

I always felt very happy when my Grandfather would tell the neighbors that I could make good biscuits. I treasured praise from my Grandfather, the well-loved patriarch of our small community of homesteading relatives as well as the larger community of neighbors. I remember one time when I was not proud, when the pan of golden brown biscuits came from the oven very flat. I had forgotten the baking powder! Nobody scolded, but I could scarcely keep the tears from squeezing out and I seemed to hurt inside.

Grandpa soaked his biscuits with milk gravy and said they were very good. I didn't forget the baking powder for years.

Before starting to prepare your biscuits or any food, assemble all your ingredients and collect all utensils.

Place **2 cups of flour** in a **medium mixing bowl.** This recipe will make enough biscuits for a family of four. Add ½ **cup lard, 1 scant teaspoon salt, 4 teaspoons of baking powder,** ½ **teaspoon soda** to the flour and work thoroughly into fine granules. Sprinkle ¾ **cup of buttermilk** over the mixture. This forms a firm but soft dough. If all the dry ingredients do not work in, gradually add a little more buttermilk.

When working with the dry ingredients, crush lumps of soda and baking powder so that no bitter tasting yellow spots spoil your biscuits. Lumps may be crushed by the back of a spoon.

Sprinkle the bread board with nearly ¼ cup of flour and turn dough onto the board. Work lightly into a ball with the tips of fingers and roll out to approximately 1-inch thick. I usually cut the biscuits with a large cutter, but for special occasions I use a two-inch cutter. If the dough seems to be sticking to the board, lift gently from the sides and add more flour. Don't forget to flour the rolling pin.

Of course, the biscuits are not really any better, but the use of my grandmother's rolling pin seems to add a special touch. This rolling pin was hand made by my grandfather for his bride on that far away day.

The biscuits may be baked on an ungreased or slightly greased cookie sheet or bread pan. Pre-heat the oven to 450°, bake 15 or 20 minutes or until they are a deep golden brown. In my yesterdays I would stick my hand into the open oven and if it seemed very hot it was ready for the biscuits.

Serve hot biscuits with butter and/or jelly, honey, or chokecherry syrup and they are good enough for an epicure.

COLD BISCUITS FOR SNACKS

Left over biscuits have many uses, but cold biscuits for snacks are delicious. One treat I especially enjoyed as a child was to open a cold biscuit, butter it generously, then add as much sugar as possible and put the top back on. Four of these biscuits packed in a little paper bag, would be a picnic lunch for my younger sister, Olive and me. With our brown paper bag we would run along a deep, winding buffalo trail — our sunbonnets dangling down our backs, and our hair flying. We would drop, panting, to the thick grass on a small prairie hill and slowly eat our biscuits. Fleecy white clouds scudded across the wide blue sky. A hawk hovered high above watching for a mouse, a gopher, or even one of the family chickens. A meadowlark balanced on a twig of a wild rose bush and eyed us inquisitively before flying away.

We licked our fingers for the last grain of sugar and the last crumb of biscuit — then slowly went home enjoying the stillness of the land.

WARMED-UP BISCUITS

The dinner menu may include buttermilk biscuits, so why not make a double batch; the left-overs to be stored in the refrigerator in plastic bags. Stored in this manner, biscuits will be usable for at least a week. If a person is really ambitious several dozen biscuits could be made, cooked and frozen.

Unexpected guests will be delighted with hot biscuits for lunch or dinner. Place the cold biscuits in a brown paper sack in a 325 degree oven and heat for fifteen minutes. If the biscuits seem to be rather dry, sprinkle very lightly with water or spread with butter before putting in the oven. If you sprinkle them with water it will be necessary to heat for at least twenty minutes. I suggest you adjust your oven and the time to give the effect of fresh biscuits as ovens do differ. Frozen biscuits are reheated in the same manner but it will take a few minutes longer to heat properly for serving. Times are approximate, for people and ovens differ. Warmed-up biscuits are as good as the freshly baked ones and are a time saver for a busy cook.

BREADED TOMATOES

Another favorite food of homestead days was breaded tomatoes. I occasionally serve them even today, and they taste just as good as they did when I was a little girl. **A pound can of whole tomatoes** will serve four or five people.

Bring the tomatoes to a boil; add a **tablespoon of butter, 2 teaspoons sugar,** and **some pepper and perhaps some salt** if necessary. Just before serving, break **two or three cold biscuits** into approximately two-inch pieces and drop into the tomatoes and juice. If there is not enough liquid on the tomatoes, add a little water. Stir gently to mix the biscuits with the juice and when completely soaked, the breaded tomatoes are ready to serve. Use either a vegetable bowl or individual serving dishes.

Add diced zucchini to the tomatoes for a piquant change in flavor. **Crisply fried bacon** crumbled over the tomatoes just before serving makes another variation.

DRESSING MADE WITH BISCUITS

As I remember the dressing Mamma prepared when she planned to serve chicken or turkey was much superior to any served in a restaurant or in fact any dressing that I have ever eaten. It was a "must" in her cooking methods to always use biscuits for dressing. If she did not have biscuits on hand, she would bake a big batch the night before. I remember how good those piping-hot biscuits smelled when Mamma took them from the oven, but I was not allowed to eat even one because there might not be enough for the dressing. We only had dressing when we had company for dinner, and there were enough relatives to set a first and second table so Mamma made enough dressing to serve 15 to 20 people.

Mamma broke each biscuit into several chunks in a big bowl. Next she **diced the onions** over the bread, and sprinkled the mixture with **salt, pepper, sage,** and **1 teaspoon baking powder.** To this she poured the **juices or basting liquid** from the chicken or turkey. It was usually a big roasting hen or two or maybe three as turkeys were scarce in those days. If there was not enough liquid to saturate the bread she added **hot water and a big piece of butter.** The bread must be *well-moistened* but not runny.

Today, if I do not have enough liquid from the fowl, I use bouillon and butter or margerine. I obtain some liquid by placing the neck and giblets and 4 cups of water into the pressure cooker, and cook for 30 minutes at 15 pound pressure. I may add some butter to this liquid if the bird is not fat.

Mamma seldom stuffed the bird, but baked the dressing in a bread pan for about thirty minutes in a hot oven while the meat was getting a final browning and fresh biscuits were baking. The dressing came from the oven crispy brown and although it did not have enough baking powder to make it raise, it was neither heavy or soggy. In fact, it had a fluffy texture, and was very, very good eating.

I usually make dressing by the "guess and taste" method, and looked in several cookbooks to get some proportions, but I could find no recipe for baked dressing. There were a few recipes for stuffing, but the proportions would not be quite the same as the stuffing picks up some moisture from the fowl. This also makes the meat drier.

I carefully measured all ingredients and the following recipe will serve 6 to 8 people if they aren't greedy. Place **6 to 8 cups buttermilk biscuits** broken into ¼ to ½ inch pieces in a **4-quart mixing bowl**. Dice the **giblets and** add to bread. Use ¼ to ½ cup diced onion (according to how well a person enjoys cooked onions). **Salt** may or may not be required depending on the amount of salt already in the bread and liquid. Sprinkle on ¼ **to** ½ **teaspoon of sage,** ¼ **to** ½ **teaspoon black pepper, 1 teaspoon baking powder.** These seasonings are all relative to the individual or family preference. Gradually pour in **3 to 4 cups broth** — or enough to make the mixture quite moist but not runny.

Be especially careful with the sage as it is sometimes very strong and then an average amount would make the dressing almost bitter. Put in a small amount of seasoning and if you enjoy mild flavors that may be enough, or you may like zesty flavors, so add some more seasoning. Mix and taste until you have just the right savory combination. Grease a 9" x 12" baking pan, and pour in the dressing. Bake in a hot oven for 25 to 30 minutes.

PORK STEAK AND DRESSING

This dressing recipe is excellent as a stuffing for pork chops or between pork steaks. I brown the pork steaks on one side, turn and place a serving of the dressing on the browned side, and another steak on top of the dressing with the cooked side down. Sprinkle the steak with salt or garlic salt and some black pepper. Bake in 425 degree oven for 20 to 30 minutes. Serve immediately.

These steaks make large individual meat servings for an excellent dinner served with a vegetable, a tossed salad and assorted fruits for dessert.

STRAWBERRY SHORTCAKE

Buttermilk biscuits, in my opinion, are tops for the cake part of strawberry shortcake.

Split the biscuits and butter, place on a cookie sheet and just before time for serving, heat in a 400 degree oven. When the butter is melted and the biscuits slightly browned, take from oven and top with whole sweetened strawberries and serve with either thick cream or whipped cream. The crunchy toasted biscuit is a savory complement to the strawberries, and more tasty than any type of cake.

LIGHTBREAD

The yeasty smell of baking lightbread is a tantalizing aroma and makes all those that are near very hungry. We who were children in homestead days were no exception and seldom ventured far from the tar-papered shack on baking day, for we could hardly wait for the big, brown loaves to cool enough for slicing. The one whose turn it was to get the crispy end crust was considered the fortunate child.

Making lightbread in the early days was a tedious and long drawn-out process. First the yeast must be set or the "rising set" and this was an evening chore. If there were boiled potatoes for supper **two or three potatoes** were saved. Into a large container we put the **water and mashed potatoes, adding warm water** to make two or three quarts of liquid. To this we added **two or three cakes of hard dry yeast** (yeast foam) and **enough flour** to make a batter slightly thicker than pancake dough. These hard dry yeast cakes were much the same size as the Fleischmann yeast cakes of today. They were packed six to a package, and retained their potency indefinitely.

The "rising" slowly began to bubble, and was stirred down when bedtime came and left to rise overnight. The next morning sufficient flour was added to make a very stiff dough and was kneaded for at least 20 minutes. This dough was let rise and was worked down twice and on the third rising was shaped into loaves and placed in bread pans. Mamma generally made two pans of bread with four loaves to a pan. One was a long pan about the size of cookie sheet, which Olive now has.

I have the square one and both of us still use them occasionally.

The variety of wheat used for flour during the early part of the century made the technique of baking bread entirely different from that used today.

It was difficult to keep the rising from freezing in the winter on the homestead. Heating stoves and cook-stoves were banked at night to hold the fire, but at times the house became very cold. The coals would burn down and turn red with no flames showing. A grownup put 2 or 3 large chunks of coal in the front room stove, and smaller chunks in the kitchen stove, allowed the fire to start to burn slightly, then almost closed the damper in the stove pipe, and closed the drafts in the fire box. Unless there was a high wind, the fire would smolder all night.

In the morning, the damper and drafts were opened, the grates shaken, and soon the fire burned briskly.

On a cold winter night, Mamma would wrap the yeast rising in blankets and put in the open oven to keep warm. Some people even took the rising to bed with them. I always wondered how they kept from spilling it.

Mamma made many things from the basic lightbread dough. Among these of course the delicious bread, coffee cake, doughnuts, fried twists, rolls, cinnamon rolls.

The following is an excellent foundation recipe for bread making. I use a 6-quart bowl and place in the bowl **4 cups quite warm tap water, ¼ cup of sugar or ¼ cup honey, 4 cups flour** and **2 tablespoons of dry granulated yeast.** I sometimes use Baker's yeast using the equivalent amount in proportion to the dry yeast. Baker's yeast may be obtained at a bakery and a pound is quite reasonable. The bread seems to have a more yeasty flavor which I like. Baker's yeast is soft and moist.

I stir the mixture and let stand for a few minutes until the yeast starts to work, add **2 tablespoons salt** and **¼ cup shortening** then add **4 cups of unsifted flour** and stir well. I now divide the dough into two equal parts if I plan to make coffee cake. Set one-half aside for the coffee cake and make up the bread first. (If you only plan to make bread, do not divide dough and add 6½ cups flour.)

The divided dough is not stiff enough to knead, so I add one cup of flour, stir and turn out on a lightly floured bread board. It may be that some more flour may be needed but that depends a great deal on the accuracy of the measurements and the texture of the flour. The dough should be moist. In fact it is almost sticky, but should not stick to the hands or board. It should not flatten out but retain a rounded shape.

The cook, to understand this rather ambiguous statement must actually make a batch of bread and experiment with the dough's consistency. The dough must be kneaded for approximately 10 to 15 minutes. The kneading process is really easy. The dough is ball shaped. Push down hard with the heel of the hand, away from the body while pulling the dough toward the body with curved fingers, meanwhile rotate it either to the left or right. Continue working by punching down hard with the heel of the hand, or the fist working from the center to the outside, turning over and rotating. Keep the board lightly floured so the material will not pick up too much flour. After kneading for a short time cut through the dough with a sharp knife and check for holes. If there are big holes, keep kneading hard and checking until the holes are of a minimum size.

Grease the mixing bowl, and grease the dough by turning and rolling in the bowl, cover and set aside to rise in a place out of drafts and at room temperature. It may double in bulk anywhere from 45 minutes to an hour and a half.

Thoroughly knead and allow to double in bulk again.

Divide into two parts, then knead, roll hard into a ball shape, lengthen out, fold under. Work again, continuing the process until the dough is very compact. Shape into a loaf and place into a greased one pound bread pan. Let rise for 20 or 30 minutes or until nearly double in bulk. If raising at room temperature it will rise rapidly and at the end of that time will be ready to go into a 300° preheated oven, where it will continue to rise until it is a well-rounded loaf.

After 10 minutes turn heat up to 325° and bake for 30 to 35 minutes when the bread should have a tender and beautiful golden crust. To check if the bread is done, turn pan on side on a platter or a bread board and pull out loaf. Touch the bread lightly on the side and if the crust springs back quickly it is done. If there is a dent where the finger touched, return the bread to the oven for a few more minutes and check again. If the bread is not as brown as you wish and you have 10 minutes to go, raise the temperature to 350°.

Other methods of checking for doneness is to thump the top crust with your finger. If it has a hollow sound, it is done. Another indication of doneness is the pulling away of the bread from the side of the pan.

If the crust, by chance, is too hard after removal from oven, leave loaf in pan for a few minutes. Steam will help soften the lower crust slightly. To soften the top crust, grease with butter and cover with a doubled cloth for a short time. Then place on rack to cool.

I like a slice of this fresh hot bread, dripping with butter, a glass of cold milk, and several little green onions.

COFFEE CAKE

I remember cool Saturday afternoons in late fall or winter waiting for the coffee cake to come from the oven. Two small girls — both blond, one with blue eyes and curls, the other with long heavy plaits and brown eyes sitting by the scrubbed kitchen table hungrily waiting for the combination smell of lightbread and carmalized brown sugar to come from the oven. Oh, that delicious coffee cake! We were allowed one slice apiece fresh from the oven. Then we could scrape the gobs of brown sugar and butter frosting from the pans.

I gave a basic recipe for four loaves of bread. If this recipe is divided while in the soft dough stage, it will make three coffee cakes and two loaves of bread. To one-half of the sponge or soft dough add ¼ **cup of sugar, 2 eggs slightly beaten, and 1½ cups more flour.** Stir and turn onto a well-floured bread board.

The added sugar and eggs may make this mixture rather sticky, and it may be necessary to gradually add more flour, until the dough will not stick to the hands or board. Knead and work alternately for approximately 10 minutes or until there are no big air holes when cut with a sharp knife. Shape into a ball and let rise until double in bulk, then knead again right in the bowl. Set the oven on bake at 300 degrees, and grease three cake pans. Divide the dough in three parts, work into a ball, place in cake pans and spread to the edge of the pan, making a slight depression about five inches across the center. Hopefully this will keep the coffee cake from bulging in the middle while baking. Allow to rise until almost double and place in oven. After 10 minutes turn oven to 325°.

— The bread and coffee cake may bake at the same time. The coffee cake cooks more quickly as it is thinner. I sometimes set the oven to 350° to finish cooking the bread.

COFFEE CAKE FROSTING

When the cakes are a very light brown, add the brown sugar frosting. Cream **1 cup of brown sugar** and **½ cup of butter.** Add **cream 1** teaspoonful at a time and mix until there is a thick paste. Spread generously over the coffee cake, sprinkle with **cinnamon** and return to oven, baking for 10 to 15 minutes or until the frosting is candied. No wonder my sister and I didn't stray far from the kitchen when coffee cake was baking!

This cake is delicious for breakfast, brunch, lunch or supper.

CINNAMON LOAF

Another family favorite that is made from the basic bread recipe is a cinnamon roll made in loaf style.

Take one-fourth of the basic lightbread recipe and gently pat it out to approximately 18 to 24 inches long and as wide as the length of a one pound loaf pan. **Spread butter** generously over the dough, **sprinkle with brown sugar and cinnamon.** The amount you use depends on your liking for sweets and spices. **Raisins and currants** give an additional touch that is delicious, so scatter a handful of either one or both over the cinnamon and sugar. Now roll the dough from the end until the loaf is formed. Pinch the edges tightly together and place into a greased bread pan. Pat the dough down until it is level. Use a sharp knife and cut through the raw dough making one-half to three-fourths inch thick slices.

Sometimes I butter the top of the loaf and sprinkle with brown sugar and cinnamon. This is optional to the individual. Cover and let rise for twenty minutes or until nearly double in bulk at room temperature and place in a preheated 300 degree oven and turn to 325 degrees in 10 minutes. It is well to note here that if the bread is rising at room temperature and has been handled properly, 20 minutes is plenty of time for the loaf to rise. Another thing to remember is that the first kneading of the bread is not sufficient, and the second time knead again thoroughly, then prepare for the baking pan.

After the dough has baked for 20 minutes, start a fresh percolator of coffee, and call your next door neighbor. Tell her cinnamon loaf will be served in 20 minutes. When she arrives, she will be greeted by the fragrance of perking coffee and the tantalizing smell of fresh cooked bread with the spicy smell of cinnamon and brown sugar.

Hand your neighbor a pie plate, and a fork and say "HELP YOUR-SELF." Insert the fork into the previously sliced portions of the loaf and it will divide easily into generous portions.

FRIED LIGHTBREAD

If the bread baking was coming on slowly as it did occasionally when the weather was quite cold or Mamma got a slow start with her bread or the quality of the yeast was poor and we had no bread for supper, Mamma would take balls of raw dough about two inches thick, pat them into thin biscuits, let raise a few minutes and then fry. When both sides of the biscuits were fried a crispy brown, and served with chokeberry jelly or syrup they were a very tasty change from light-bread. These fried lightbread biscuits were good rolled in sugar while still hot.

From the basic lightbread recipe, Mamma would make dinner rolls, large flat buns for sandwiches, conventional cinnamon rolls or any other desired variation.

Most of the modern sweetbreads have sugar, eggs and milk added to the dough. All of these ingredients could be used with the basic bread recipe, but it would probably be necessary to add some additional flour to compensate for the extra moisture. I like these sweet breads and sometime use them, but the combination of the sweet bread and the frosting may become satiating.

I really prefer the contrast of the regulation bread and the sweet-ness of the various types of fillings and frostings.

SUGAR TWISTS

I have a variety of things that I do with the basic bread recipe. One that Mamma made and Olive and I especially liked when we were little girls was sugar twists.

Use a fourth of the standard recipe; roll or pat out in an oblong shape, ½ inch thick, 12" wide and as long as possible. Cut the dough into 1" strips, 12" long. Shape the strip into an upside down U, then cross the dough, alternating from left to right or right to left whichever is most convenient. When the twist is completed, fasten the ends together with a toothpick through the last twist to keep from spreading. Allow the twists to rise 10 to 15 minutes at room temperature, then drop into deep fat. (Try the fat first by dropping in scraps of dough.) When they fry to a golden brown on the underside the grease is hot enough.

Mamma had a black-handled fork with four sharp tines that she used in turning the twists. When both sides were brown, she held up the twist to allow the fat to drip off, then rolled it in white sugar to coat.

We seldom were allowed more than one apiece of these sugared goodies when they were fresh from the pan, but my they were good! We ate them very slowly, savoring each tender, sugary morsel — then finally licking our sugary fingers.

The twists were made only for special occasions — for school treats, for picnics or for company.

TO BAKE A RHUBARB PIE

When I want applause and approbation from the men of my family, I bake a rhubarb pie. When the steaming pie with softly browned crust and bright red juices spewing from the vents is taken from the oven any member of the family in the house gathers round to "Ah" and "Oh" and beg for just a taste. How do I make this pie?

If possible, gather the rhubarb fresh from the garden early in the morning before the sun's rays have become sweltering. Rhubarb leaves are poisonous so be careful. Thoroughly scrub the stalks, and cut into ¼" lengths. I use approximately **4 heaping cups of rhubarb.** Blend **2 cups of sugar, 4 tablespoons of flour** and **2 slightly beaten eggs** and mix with the rhubarb. If I am using the Canadian red or strawberry rhubarb, the juices will be a deep, ruby red. I set this mixture aside for the juices to form while I make the crust.

PIE CRUST

My favorite pie crust recipe must be well over 100 years old as it was used by my grandmother during and following the Civil War period. As mentioned previously, I use her rolling pin, hand-turned on a lathe by my grandfather.

The actual crust recipe is **1 cup of flour** for one double crust pie, **½ cup of lard,** and **¼ cup of water.** The simple directions is to half each ingredient according to the amount of flour used. There is also a dash of salt, which could be simplified to **¼ teaspoon of salt.**

I find a four-pronged fork excellent for working the lard into the flour. A pastry blender is a gadget worth having. When fine granules have been formed, sprinkle with water and stir gently until the mixture forms a ball. Knead half this dough lightly into a smooth ball. Do not overwork pie crust as it becomes tough. Roll out the dough 1/8 inch thick and large enough to extend an inch beyond the edges of a 9" pan.

Tender dough is hard to handle; fold the dough over, bring the pie pan next to the doubled side, gently slip both hands under the dough and place in the pie pan with doubled edge on center line of pan. Unfold the dough so the entire pan is covered loosely. Trim the edges so they extend evenly ½ inch beyond pan, then roll the top crust. Fold the top crust and make a design by slitting the dough with the tip of a sharp knife. Start the slit ½ inch away from the double, and cut through both layers of dough.

It might be fun to be original and start a family tradition by making your own design. Daughter Pearl makes "Merry Christmas," "Happy Birthday" or even names. Our family uses this design which has been followed for at least four generations. I simply make parallel inch slits on a diagonal away from the fold.

When the top pie crust is ready, turn back to the rhubarb mixture which has become quite juicy. Grease the lower crust lightly by rubbing with butter or lard to prevent sogginess and pour in the rhubarb mixture. Dampen the edges of the lower crust, put the top crust in place and trim so it is one-half inch bigger than the lower crust. Hold upright. Fold the top crust one-half inch over the bottom crust pressing firmly together and flute with the fingers. This may be fluted by twisting between thumb and forefinger, or two forefingers and thumb, or even designs with a fork. You may figure out other flutings. Place the pie in a 450 degree oven and bake 10 minutes, then lower heat to 375 degrees and bake for 35 to 40 minutes.

The rhubarb pie is now ready to serve, if you like your pie hot, otherwise cool it for an hour.

Apple pie does not have a corner on cheese and a tasty piece of a favorite cheese may be added to the serving plate. I prefer a mild type.

If there is danger of juices running over, put aluminum foil or a cookie sheet under the pie so you won't have burnt juice in your oven.

If the crust is becoming too brown, cover lightly with a piece of aluminum foil.

Pearl had a blue ribbon rhubarb pie at the Fair one winter. After the judging, the pies are auctioned to help defray expenses. John bought his sister's pie, because he didn't want a stranger to buy it, and eat that blue-ribbon pie.

OTHER RHUBARB RECIPES

At the edge of the garden Grandpa had 3 or 4 clumps of rhubarb. He kept them well fertilized and they produced abundantly. We had rhubarb sauce, rhubarb cobbler, rhubarb and strawberry jam, rhubarb and apricot jam, rhubarb pie, and canned rhubarb sauce. When cooking rhubarb, remember that you add a very small amount of liquid, as it is so very juicy.

When making rhubarb sauce, add a **small amount of salt** which helps to cut the tartness, **add just enough water so it will not scorch** and simmer until done, only a few minutes — then add enough **sugar** to sweeten. If you use **4 cups of diced rhubarb,** you will need **1 cup of sugar,** possibly more.

RHUBARB AND DUMPLINGS

If you want to try rhubarb and dumplings use — **2 cups of water, 1 quart of diced rhubarb,** and **2 cups of sugar.** I use only ½ the recipe for dumplings and drop by teaspoon instead of tablespoons.

RHUBARB WINE

Rhubarb wine is another treat. Wash **five pounds of rhubarb,** chop into inch chunks and pound well. Put in stone jar and add **1 gallon of water.** Cover and let stand for 9 days. Drain off the liquid and strain.

To this liquid add **3 pounds sugar, 1 ounce of ginger root,** (ginger root may be obtained at some grocery stores) and the **juice of 1 lemon.** Let this stand until it quits working and place in jars or bottles and cap. Keep stored in a cool place.

Note — "Working" means that the liquid is turning to wine. Bubbles will rise to the surface.

If you like a sweet wine, use 4½ pounds of sugar.

"PUDDIN' BACK"

The recipe "Puddin' Back" was a favorite dessert many years before the exodus of the Romine family westward. It was popular during homestead days and still is with the many branches of the family today.

Guests arrived at the big white two-story home set far back on the sloping well trimmed lawn. Visiting and news exchanging was conducted in hushed whispers, — "Had Eliza had her baby yet?" "Did Cousin Ben still have rheumatism?" "Was Helen going to school?" — as the generous dinner was eaten. Uncle Sid was then only half-grown and was not particularly interested in family conversation and finally blurted out, "Ma, is there any 'puddin' back'?" There was general laughter as my grandmother returned from the pantry with my uncle's favorite dessert, bread pudding. But "puddin' back" became a much-used expression in the family for any type of dessert.

When I was small we were many times served different versions of bread pudding and the following recipe with it's accompanying sauce became a family tradition.

There is no resemblance between the bread pudding I serve and the soggy, solid replacement sometimes served in restaurants.

This is the recipe I use — one that we like — but still never as good as the pudding my mother made. The following proportions will serve 8 to 10 people. Tear sufficient **lightbread** or **biscuits** into small pieces to make **4 firmly packed cups.** I prefer biscuits so the texture of the pudding will not be soggy.

Empty the bread chunks into a medium size mixing bowl, add **4½ cups of milk, 3 large or 4 medium eggs** slightly beaten, **1 cup white sugar or brown sugar,** well packed. (Brown sugar will give a richer flavor.) Use **1 teaspoon of vanilla flavoring** and **½ teaspoon of soda.** Finally stir in **2 cups of diced rhubarb,** more if you are very fond of rhubarb, which gives a zesty tang to the pudding. Pour this mixture into either a round, square or oblong pan that has been lightly greased.

The baking dish should approximate a 9" by 11" pan and be at least 3" deep. There is not enough soda to make the pudding rise, but it helps to counteract the acidity of the rhubarb. The oven should be preheated from 350 degrees to 375 degrees depending on the altitude. The higher the altitude the higher the temperature. The baking time will be from 45 minutes to 1 hour, and when done the pudding will resemble a firm custard. One method of checking doneness is to insert a knife blade and if it comes out clean, the pudding is done. Mamma always said to use a silver knife, but I find that stainless steel works just as well.

PUDDING SAUCE

This dessert is made more delicious by adding a specially cooked sauce. Cream **1 cup sugar** and **¼ cup butter** or **½ cup butter** if you want a very rich sauce. Work into this combination either **4 tablespoons flour or cornstarch.** Slowly stir in **one cup boiling water.** Cook slowly stirring constantly, over low heat until the sauce thickens and begins to clear. I prefer using a double boiler. It is necessary to stir, but not as much. Flavor with **1 teaspoon lemon extract or lemon juice** to taste.

If you want a really thick sauce, use one cup of boiling water; add more water to make a thinner sauce, and the type depends on the individual or family. I prefer the thick sauce. If you have some **sweet red rhubarb sauce** on hand, spoon over each serving of bread pudding before adding the lemon sauce. This makes an outstanding dessert — both for taste and appearance.

Raisins or dried apples may be substituted for the rhubarb and for a special treat, **blueberries** may be used.

A different version of the sauce would be to use brown sugar and substitute ½ cup of orange juice for water. When making the sauce experiment with blueberry syrup or rum or rum extract just to get the gourmet touch.

I enjoy the pudding warm from the oven and the sauce hot from the stove as a hearty dessert on a cool evening.

This pudding is also excellent served cold as a snack if any is left over — for then there will be some "puddin' back" for Uncle Sid, small Johnny, Stephanie and Michael, or the hungry children coming home from school.

PLANTING THE GARDEN

Olive and I were enthusiastic helpers when the garden was planted in the spring. At least we thought we helped and we were allowed to plant some of the seeds.

Garden preparations began the fall before. Grandpa cleaned the garden spot in the fall and had several loads of barn manure spread over the ground. As soon as the frost was gone in the spring, the soil was plowed, harrowed and dragged. Grandpa saved many of the seeds from the vegetables in the fall. Sometime in late February or early March, he would test them by placing rows of seeds on a cloth maybe 6 or 8 inches wide and several inches long. He would roll up the cloth, dampen it and let stand in a warm dark place for a few days. He then checked

the seeds for germination.

As I remember, these rolls of seeds and cloth were called dolleys. I couldn't see the resemblance, but I didn't argue the matter.

Additional seeds were ordered from Will's Seed House at Mandan, North Dakota.

Olive and I very eagerly watched the growing garden and sometimes tested to see if the plants were big enough to eat, which generally led to orders to stay out of the garden. We felt aggrieved, not realizing that small shoe prints in the cultivated soil and wilted vegetables between the rows pointed out the trespassers.

BEETS

Olive and James always had bright rosy cheeks, and they both liked beets very much, so we teased them by saying all the beets they ate made their rosy cheeks.

Just as soon as the little beets were as big as tiny marbles, Grandpa or Mamma began to thin them, so the remainder of the beets would have space to grow.

BEET GREENS

Mamma washed the beets and leaves thoroughly, snipped off the roots, placed them in a large kettle with a cup of boiling water and cooked them until tender. Those tiny beets, stems and leaves made very tasty greens, when drained and served hot. They might be seasoned with some hot bacon grease and salt, or a few drops of vinegar.

Beet greens, boiled potatoes fried, either fried ham or bacon, and hot corn bread made a hearty and nutritious supper — with the beet greens the main attraction.

Radish tops, dandelions (before they bloom) and wild mustard, turnip tops and rutabaga tops all make good greens, and are also good mixed. It is always well to pick them when they are young, so they will not be strong tasting and tough.

BUTTERED BEETS

When the beets become dollar size, they can be cooked without the tops. The tops may be used separately as greens. Cut the tops from the beets leaving at least two inches of stem, to prevent color bleeding of the beets. Cook the beets until tender, drain off the hot water, add cold water and allow to cool enough to handle. The skins and stems slip off easily when rubbed by the hand. **Slice the beets, season with 2 or 3 tablespoons of butter, and sprinkle with salt.** Return to stove and keep warm until time for serving.

Beets are very edible when cooked in this manner even when two or three or even more inches in diameter.

BEET PICKLES

Pickled beets may be prepared from any size beets you may prefer.

Boil the beets, remove the skins, then dice, quarter, or slice. The pickling solution is made by using the proportion of **1 cup water, 1 cup vinegar, 1 cup sugar, 1 teaspoon salt for 2 quarts of pickles.**

Put the liquid necessary for the number of quarts you plan to pickle in a large kettle, leaving enough space for your beets, bring to boil, add the beets and boil for twenty minutes. Can in sterilized jars, according to the directions with the jars when purchased.

I sometimes pickle small whole beets which makes a very attractive pickle. If you like highly-seasoned pickles put a tablespoon of pickling spices in four quarts of beets while pickling. They may either be put in loose, or put in a small cotton bag. I usually do not bother with the bag as I like the spices mixed with the beets.

A meat platter decorated with small pickled beets and pickled onions makes a colorful main dish.

Beet relish served with meats is excellent during the winter months. I remember the grinding and grinding of beets and the drip, drip of the dark red juice into a pan when Mamma was going to make beet relish. She diced celery, and chopped cabbage while I ground beets. She canned several quarts for winter use, but you might want to make just a few pints the first time.

BEET RELISH

Here are two good beet relish recipes:

#1 4 cups coarse ground or diced cooked beets
   (the diced makes a more attractive relish)
   4 cups chopped or grated cabbage
   2 cups diced celery
   1 tablespoon salt
   3 cups sugar
   1½ cups vinegar
   1½ cups water
   1 teaspoon celery seed
   ½ teaspoon turmeric

Bring the mixture to a boil, and cook slowly for 30 minutes. Can in sterilized pint jars. If there is not enough liquid to come to the top of the beet mixture for the last can or two, add sufficient water and vinegar plus a little more sugar to the cooking relish, bring to boil and boil 3 minutes, then continue canning.

#2 The second beet relish recipe, contains all the ingredients of the above recipe plus:
   ¼ cup ground or grated fresh horseradish and
   ¼ teaspoon red pepper
   Cooking time is the same.

CARROTS, CARROTS AND MORE CARROTS

Grandpa planted several rows of carrots. He liked the oxhart which is short, stubby and very fat looking, and another kind was very long and also got big across the top.

We liked to slip into the garden when no one was looking, just as soon as the carrots were at all edible and pull out some to eat. We always carefully hid the tops, and wiped off the dirt on our aprons. We didn't want to go to the house to wash the carrots or Mamma would know we had been in the garden. Now, I know she didn't really care, as long as we were careful and didn't destroy anything.

When the carrots got bigger, Mamma began to thin them and boil the little whole carrots. Sometimes these boiled carrots would be seasoned just a little with **butter, salt and pepper.** As they grew, Mamma peeled and sliced them, and either just used the butter, salt and pepper seasoning or creamed them. After they were done she added 2 **tablespoons butter, 1 teaspoon salt, and ¼ teaspoon pepper and 2 cups of milk to a quart of sliced carrots then added thickener.** Usually some liquid was left in the kettle. This was not poured off and the milk added to it.

Other times Mamma drained the sliced carrots and put them in the big skillet in 2 tablespoons of hot melted butter. She stirred occasion-

ally until the carrots were lightly brown; then served them. This was my favorite carrot dish, except carrot pie.

CARROT PRESERVES

The deep, shiny orange of carrot preserves in a clear glass jar is very attractive on the pantry shelf. What is more, it is just as palatable as its appearance indicates.

Aunt Ella concocted the carrot preserves and I still remember when she brought a jar to Mamma — that beautiful orange color, those small carefully diced bits of carrots in the heavy amber juice, and the intriguing taste as we all sampled the new kind of preserves. Aunt Ella was always interested in making something new, something artistically different. Aunt Ella added dignity to any occasion — her erect slender figure and beautiful white hair piled high on her head.

Take **8 cups of diced or ground raw carrots. Add 4 cups water,** bring to a boil, and cook slowly stirring often until almost tender. It may be necessary to add more water as it will probably take ½ hour or more to cook the carrots.

When almost tender **add ½ cup vinegar or ½ cup lemon juice, 4 cups sugar,** and stir well. Then add enough water to just come to the top of the carrots. It will take an hour or more to finish cooking the preserves, perhaps longer, as it is necessary to cook them very slowly. Stir often to prevent scorching. Cook the carrots until the juice is very thick — much like a very thick honey, then add **2 teaspoons lemon extract,** and can in ½ pint sterilized jars or in jelly glasses.

If you desire variety, **add 1/2 teaspoon cinnamon, 1/8 teaspoon cloves, and 1/8 teaspoon allspice.**

SUMMER ON THE PRAIRIES

Summer meant day after day of bright, hot sunlight — but pleasantly cool nights. Tall grasses waved as swift winds rushed across the plains.

Sometimes we heard the quick whir of the prairie chicken's wings, or the soft quacking of small ducks on the sloughs.

When a careless person dropped a match or threw out ashes, a dreaded prairie fire would grow frighteningly big, to be battled by homesteaders that came many miles to save the land. Finally, it was quenched at the river's edge. But, the rains would come, and new grasses would grow.

Each season brought new hope, new courage — there would be a good crop next year.

LET'S HAVE STEWED TURTLE

We were visiting at Uncle Bert's one summer when Uncle John was there. Uncle John never wanted to miss out on any kind of fun or visiting. He and Uncle Bert discovered a large land turtle and decided that it was edible.

Aunt Hattie was very reluctant to have the turtle in her kitchen, but she told them she would cook it if they would dress it. They came in with 3 or 4 pounds of turtle meat. Aunt Hattie stewed this until it was tender and seasoned it with **butter, salt,** and **pepper** and **some thickener.**

She fried some very good steaks and the rest of us ate steak while Uncle Bert and Uncle John enjoyed the turtle stew.

I sampled the turtle meat — it had a mild taste and the texture of the meat was firm. It really was all right, but I must be a creature of habit, as I prefer steak.

WILD FRUITS OF THE PLAINS

In late June or early July, the June berries ripened on tall, slender bushes. We hunted for the berries in the coal bank coulee which stretched from near Cousin Lillie's homestead west toward the Little Muddy and the Reservation. Sometimes we went to the coulees near Elsie's homestead.

Both these coulees were within walking distance so we children were allowed to go by ourselves to hunt for the sweet June berries. We took Jum, our black and white shepherd dog, a syrup pail with water and other pails to carry the berries. Sometimes we would be gone for hours.

We wandered over the hills, hunted meadow lark nests, peeked at the eggs or baby birds, picked up pretty rocks, gathered June berries. We ate just about as many berries as we put in the pails. We also located the pin cushion cactus and the prickly pear, planning to go back later to eat the cactus berries.

The cactus blossoms were beautiful — especially the prickly pear. Their large flowers were a deep satin yellow that glistened in the sunlight. The pin cushion cactus blossoms were a soft pinkish lavendar, much smaller than the prickly pear blossoms but with that rich satiny finish. After a few encounters with either cactus we quickly developed a deep respect for their thorns. Even the little pin cushions had stickers long enough to go through a shoe sole, if it happened to be old and thin.

We sat on a hill side, and ate our cold biscuits, either with butter and sugar, or maybe some bacon or ham left over from breakfast. Jum sat beside us patiently waiting for scraps of food. He always had his share and the last of the water.

Jum was a gentle dog, but we were never worried when he was with us, because he would not back down for any animal. He chased the gophers and an occasional rabbit, but never got far away.

We gathered sprays of ground cedar to take home and found the wild sweet peas, in various shades of yellow and purple. The acres and acres of blue bells seemed to match the deep blue of the summer sky.

Finally, we would get home with our berries; tired, redfaced and hot, but happy.

We had dinner and dessert, which was June berries, sugar and cream.

SERVICE BERRY OR JUNE BERRY PIE

June berries are a mild flavor, and are only good cooked or canned if some lemon juice or vinegar is added to lessen the flatness. If you want a good pie though, take **1½ cups June berries, the same amount of ripe gooseberries** (green gooseberries are acceptable) **1 cup of sugar,** with **2 tablespoons flour** and **1 beaten egg.** Make a two crust pie and bake for 45 minutes. (If you like a sweet dessert, add another half cup sugar.)

The prairies have given us another delicious food!

RICE FOR EVERYBODY

Dan was born in Montana, the son of Aunt Hattie and Uncle Bert Romine. Dan, as a toddler, was very fond of rice. Grandpa teased him about that fondness but that didn't keep Dan from liking and eating rice.

Boiled rice makes either a breakfast or dinner dish. One satisfactory way to cook rice is to cover **2 cups rice with 6 cups boiling water** and boil gently or simmer for 2 to 3 hours, depending on the variety of rice and the amount of doneness required. I like rice tender and fluffy. I **add 2 tablespoons butter to the water** which helps to prevent it from boiling over. I stir occasionally to prevent sticking and scorching. **Add a teaspoon salt** the last few minutes of cooking.

BOILED RICE

Rice is good for breakfast served as a hot cereal with sugar and milk or cream. It is also good with just brown sugar and butter or honey and butter topping the hot cereal with a sprinkling of cinnamon added. The heat melts the topping and it dribbles down through the rice to make a mouth watering combination.

RICE AND GRAVY

If you have a big bowl of rice in the refrigerator and have unexpected company for dinner — put the rice in the double boiler to reheat.

DRIED BEEF GRAVY

Shred very fine **2 cups dried beef. Simmer in 3 cups boiling water** for several minutes.

Melt **4 tablespoons butter in a large skillet,** work in **6 tablespoons flour** and stir as it browns. Pull the skillet from the heat and add the simmering dried beef and mix thoroughly stirring constantly to keep from lumping. Add **2 or 3 cups canned or rich whole milk,** still stirring, until the ingredients are well mixed. Replace on heat and continue to stir and cook for 3 minutes.

This makes a very good gravy, rich in protein, to spoon over servings of rice, boiled potatoes, or hot biscuits. Pass the bowl of sliced beet pickles as a relish.

Deep red beets also add color contrast on the dinner plate.

Since you have rice, no bread is needed. A center piece of fresh fruit or a serving dish of cooked fruit completes a tasty meal. You may want a double batch of gravy thick with the shredded dried beef. This is a popular dish.

RICE PUDDING

A favorite of my family is rice pudding.

Beat 3 eggs 50 strokes with a fork, add 1/3 cup sugar and beat another 50 strokes. Use 2 cups well cooked rice, and 1/2 cup raisins. Stir well. Last, add 2 cups hot milk and 1 teaspoon vanilla. Pour into a slightly greased baking dish, and place in a pan with 2 or 3 inches of hot tap water. Bake in a 375° oven for approximately one hour. Check for doneness by inserting a knife blade in the center and if it comes out clean the pudding is done. Keep checking the last few minutes of cooking very carefully for if the custard part is too done water seeps from the pudding.*

Suggestions   1: – If you really want to dress up this pudding make a high peaked meringue.

2: – A half a cup raw rice is excellent added to long cooking beef broth or chicken soup.

3: – A cup of cooked rice is good in stew and quick cooking soups.

*Be a Girl Scout and take this attractive dish to your new neighbor, Dorothy B., on the corner. Watch her eyes light up as she sees this tempting dessert ready to serve for dinner or supper. It is especially appreciated as moving day has given her little time to cook, and the children will soon be home from school.

CHICKEN SOUP AND EGG NOODLES

On some occasions, Mamma had chicken soup with homemade egg noodles. She used a stewing chicken for making the soup. Sometimes she boiled the chicken whole and took off the meat after it was tender and slipped easily from the bone. Other times she cut the chicken into frying pieces, then boiled until tender. When the chicken was done, she would remove it from the soup and placed it in a pan on the back of the stove to keep warm.

Add 1 or 2 teaspoons of salt after boiling the chicken for an hour. The amount of salt depends on the size of the chicken and the amount of soup.

Bring eight cups of the soup to a hard boil, add the egg noodles and continue boiling gently for 15 minutes, at which time the soup is ready to serve. One recipe of the noodles makes a sufficient quantity for the eight cups of soup.

EGG NOODLES

To make egg noodles, beat 2 large eggs or 3 small eggs with a fork for a couple of minutes. Add 1/2 teaspoon of salt, 1/8 teaspoon of pepper, if desired, and stir in 1½ cups flour. This will make a very stiff dough. Allow to stand 30 minutes. Roll very thin. This takes some time as the dough rolls out very slowly, but keep rolling until it is thinner than pie dough. If you have made just one recipe, leave it on the bread board to dry. If you plan to double or triple, or make even more noodles, place folded dish towels over the back of the kitchen chairs and place the rolled-out dough on the cloth.

After drying the dough for an hour, cut into very small strips with a sharp knife, then cut across the strips in the desired length — perhaps 2 or 3 inches. At this time if you planned egg noodles for dinner they are ready for use. The remainder may be completely dried and stored in plastic bags or air tight containers. If you wish, they may be put in plastic bags and frozen.

Inch squares of potatoes cooked in the soup are also good. That size potatoes will take from 20 to 25 minutes to cook.

Use a large flat bottom soup dish, ladle in the soup, potatoes and noodles, add a good sized piece of chicken. There is a substantial dinner. Chunks of raw cabbage may be eaten as a relish.

One recipe of noodles cooked in 4 cups of soup is good served as a side dish or on the dinner plate. The noodles, in cooking, have absorbed practically all the liquid.

Cooked noodles are also good fried in a very small amount of butter or bacon grease. Turn often and they will become brown and crispy. Serve with stewed chicken and a large salad of some green vegetables.

DROP DUMPLINGS

There are many ways to use drop dumplings and perhaps the family favorites are with beef or chicken soup.

It is very easy to make good drop dumplings, if the directions are followed explicitely.

Sift together **2 cups flour, 1 teaspoon salt, 4 teaspoons baking powder**, and **¼ teaspoon pepper**. Add **1 well beaten egg, 3 tablespoons melted shortening and 1 cup milk**.

Reserve ¼ cup of milk when mixing the batter and check the stiffness of the dumplings. If they are very stiff, slowly add some of the milk. The dough must be moist, but stiff enough to hold its shape. It may take the entire cup of milk. This amount of batter will make 10 to 12 large dumplings.

DROP DUMPLINGS AND CHICKEN SOUP

To make chicken soup, slowly **boil in 2 to 3 quarts of water** either a whole or cut-up **stewing hen** in a large kettle. Cook for 1½ to 2 hours or until tender. The chicken would be tender enough to remove from the bone easily. Season when almost done with **salt and pepper** to taste.

Remove the chicken from the broth or soup. Drop the dumplings from a tablespoon into the boiling chicken soup. Turn the heat down so the soup and dumplings will continue to boil slowly and cover the pan tightly; cook for 18 minutes, *and do not* take the cover off the kettle while cooking. If you lift the lid, the dumplings may fall. When done, the dumplings will be moist on the outside, but will have a texture somewhat like a biscuit on the inside.

The dumplings may be placed in a large serving bowl and some of the soup poured over them. The soup in reality has turned into a gravy by the time the dumplings are done, because the cooking dough has acted as a thickener. Another way to serve is to use a large meat platter — pile the dumplings in the center, and lay pieces of chicken around the edges of the platter. Several boiled, quartered carrots placed between the dumplings make a colorful as well as a nourishing meal. Dumplings make a hearty dish for cold weather and an old expression is "They stick to the ribs."

DROP DUMPLINGS AND NEW PEAS

Boil a **quart of new peas** until nearly tender in a quart of water. Season with **1 teaspoon salt,** ¼ **teaspoon of pepper,** and **4 to 6 tablespoons of butter.**

Make up a batch of dumplings and drop by teaspoon into the boiling peas and water. Cover the kettle tightly, and turn down the heat to low or medium low, and cook 18 minutes. Add enough **evaporated milk** — perhaps half a can — to make a gravy with the peas and dumplings.

Small green onions are a suitable relish and if you want some meat, well browned fresh side pork is good. Pork chops fit in with this meal, too.

DUMPLING, SAUERKRAUT, AND PIG HOCKS

Drop dumplings with sauerkraut and pig hocks or pig shanks is a homestead dish. Sometimes you may be able to buy the pig hocks and shanks in a meat shop, but you may have to clean them yourself. It is quite a task.

Singe the hocks and shanks. Scrape well in order to get all the bristles off and be sure the skin is clean.

Simmer the meat for two or three hours or until tender. You need a big kettle or small roaster. Use at least **2 or 3 quarts of water,** for **4 hocks** or **2 hocks and 2 shanks,** or a comparative amount of meat.

Add to this liquid, after meat is tender, **two quarts of kraut,** and continue simmering for 30 more minutes. Remove the meat and place in the oven to keep warm until serving time. Drop the dumplings by tablespoon into the remaining kraut that is gently boiling in the kettle. Cover the kettle tightly and cook for 18 minutes. The heat should be turned to low. Remember *DO NOT* remove the lid until the 18 minutes are up, or the dumplings may fall.

If you are making stew on a cold winter day, make plenty of soup with your meat and vegetables, use half the dumpling recipe and drop by teaspoons into the liquid, cover tightly and cook for 12 minutes.

STRING BEANS

As I remember, I seemed to sit and string beans by the bushel when I was little. It really wasn't that bad, but I did get tired. Green beans in homestead days were called string beans because you had to string them. You would snap off one end of the bean and pull the string off one side, then snap off the other end of the bean and string the other side of the bean. Sometimes an extra string would appear. If you didn't get all those strings off, they would cook up in the beans and would still be tough hard green strings.

We strung and snapped enough beans for a large kettle nearly full, **3 or 4 quarts** at least, added just enough **water to barely cover the beans,** brought to a boil, used **4 or 5 tablespoons bacon grease,** then set back on the stove to slowly cook. Only add more water when and if beans become nearly dry. Too much liquid makes the beans watery and tasteless. A few minutes before serving, add **½ teaspoon salt for each quart of beans.** Four or 5 slices of diced raw bacon is good when cooked with the beans. If you use bacon, do not use the bacon grease.

A vegetable plate makes an excellent dinner — green beans, fried whole new potatoes, fresh cooked beets, diced and served hot with butter, salt, and pepper, radishes and green onions, and corn bread right from the oven combine to satisfy most any appetite. For guests, just add some fried home-cured ham.

As the season advances, the beans become more mature and some are big enough to shell, for the pods become too tough for good eating. When the beans are large enough for half or more to be shelled, cook a big kettle full in the same manner as the first beans of the season. They make a rich and hearty dish. They may be served without any meat, but a bit of ham or bacon adds to the flavor. With these beans, serve either sliced tomatoes or slaw from new cabbage, potatoes boiled with their jackets, milk gravy, and perhaps new onions. You won't need dessert, but choke cherry syrup over hot buttered biscuits will complete the meal in fine shape.

The bean season is over when the late fall comes and the dried pods hang in clusters from the browning vines. Olive and I gathered the beans and put them on an old canvas. We crushed the pods by walking on them and hitting them with boards. We took the corners of the canvas and flopped it up and down. The dry pods bounced out and the mature beans collected in the canvas. If it were a windy day, it was fun to scoop up pods and beans and throw in the air. The shells blew away. After hand sorting to remove bits of shell and bad beans, the dried beans were ready for winter storage.

COOKING THE MATURE DRY BEANS

Depending on the varieties of beans planted in the garden for summer use, you may have white, speckled, red, black, or brown beans.

Sort and wash **2 cups of any of these beans** and soak overnight in **6 cups of water.** The following morning bring to a boil and then set back on the stove, or turn the heat down and simmer for 1½ to 2 or more hours, or until the beans are tender. Allow them to boil almost dry. Short ribs are prime eating when boiled in these beans. The ribs should go in the kettle the same time as the beans.

Add **1 teaspoon salt** a few minutes before serving.

"Bringing in the flowers"

DRIED APPLES

I visited with Elsie the other day, and our conversation took us back a few decades to apple drying time at Grandma's and Grandpa's big white house near Gentryville, Indiana.

We both remembered that the front porch had a flat tin roof. This roof would become very hot in summer, and was easily reached by a second story window. Grandma would place her sliced apples in containers on the hot roof, cover them with cheese cloth to keep away insects and flies and leave the apples to dry beneath the hot Indiana sun. I remember Grandma gave me tastes of these brown chewy slices as a treat when she checked the drying process. When the apples became brown and leathery tough, they were ready to be stored for winter usage.

Elsie told me that in her family, she and her sister and two cousins worked together getting the apples ready to dry. One turned the apple parer, another quartered the apples, the third took out the cores and the fourth sliced the apples.

On the homestead, Mamma bought boxes of apples in the late fall, but never to dry. We had one apple apiece to eat each day. She ordered dried applies from Sears Roebuck Grocery Department and they were beautiful to see. They had been cored without quartering, and then sliced cross ways of the apple. They were big white rings and delectable to eat, but we never ate very many at a time. Olive and I were afraid they might swell up inside us, just as they did in the water when soaked overnight.

DRIED APPLE SAUCE

Dried apples are delicious when cooked. Wash the apples thoroughly, remove any blemishes, cover with cold water and soak overnight. By morning the slices will be plump, their color brown will be less brown, and much of the leathery toughness will be gone.

Place a kettle on the stove, bring apples to a slow boil, then reduce the heat to low, cover the kettle and simmer the apples until tender, an hour or longer if necessary. Add enough **sugar to sweeten. A half teaspoon of either cinnamon or nutmeg** adds to the flavor of the cooked apples.

I remember on winter mornings on the homestead we would sometimes have dried apple sauce for breakfast, and it would be partially frozen. That sauce was delicious with either a generous addition of rich milk or cream — almost apple ice cream.

We used dried apples for apple sauce, in apple pies, for jams and apple butter.

The family liked to tell this story about me. When I was about two or three years old, Grandma was in the front room resting, when I came in from the kitchen talking very emphatically about something. Grandma couldn't understand me but kept saying "yes, yes" and nodding her head. I suddenly rushed to the kitchen and returned with one of her freshly baked apple pies folded under one arm. I understand she never said "yes, yes" to me again, without understanding what I was talking about.

DRIED APPLE PIE

For one pie, cook **3 cups dried apples** until almost tender; add **½ to 1 cup sugar,** depending on the tartness of the apples, and your own taste preference. Pour into the pie crust, dot with **1 or 2 tablespoons butter** and **sprinkle with cinnamon or nutmeg.** Place on the top crust, fold the edge of the top crust under the edge of the lower crust, press firmly together and flute. Don't forget to slice holes through the top crust several times to allow for steam and juice vents. Bake for ten minutes at 425°, then lower the heat to 375° and cook 30 more minutes. You have a very tasty pie — not quite the same flavor as a fresh apple pie, but savory in its own right. Serve either hot or cold, with whipped cream, or ice cream, and be sure to place a generous piece of cheese on the serving plate.

"Mamma"

FRESH APPLE PIE

When baking a fresh apple pie, use 3½ cups of sliced apples and mix in ½ to 1 cup of sugar (adjusted to the tartness of the apples) season with preferred spices, dot with butter, and add upper crust. Cook for 10 minutes in a preheated 400° oven, then adjust the heat to 375° and cook for 45 to 50 minutes.

IMPORTANT — Baking times vary because some apples take longer to cook than others. Also some ovens are not adjusted accurately, and 375° on one oven may really be 400° or 350° in another oven. Altitude makes a difference in baking time since the higher the altitude the longer it takes for food to cook.

— If the crust is becoming too brown before the raw fruit is cooked, you may put aluminum foil over the pie, and underneath if necessary until the contents are cooked. It may take a little longer to cook with the aluminum there. Check for the doneness of the fruit by piercing with a sharp-tined fork through a vent.

The above notes apply to any type of fruit pie. I suggest you check the altitude in your neighborhood and adjust your temperatures according to that information.

ONE CRUST APPLE PIE

A two-crust apple pie is good, but I don't believe there could be a better apple pie than Mamma's one-crust sliced apple pie.

Take 4 cups of thinly sliced apples for a nine-inch pie. Mamma preferred Roman Beauty apples, when she could get them. Put 2 layers of apples in an unbaked crust; sprinkle lightly with sugar and cinnamon, and dot with butter, continue adding layers of apples and seasoning until the crust is full and slightly heaped in the center. Sprinkle the top layer with at least 2 tablespoons or more of sugar, dot liberally with butter, and sprinkle with both cinnamon and nutmeg. Dribble two tablespoons water over top of pie. I use ½ to ¾ cups of sugar, depending upon the tartness of the apples.

When done, the pie comes from the oven a tasteful, toothsome delight with a crusty surface of curling apple slices.

It is delicious hot or cold, or served with whipped cream or ice cream, or a slice of cheese.

APPLE COBBLER

An apple cobbler is a delicious hot dessert that is quickly and easily made.

Peel, core, slice and stew with 1 cup water, enough apples in a 2 quart kettle to make 3 or 4 cups apple sauce. (You may need 5 or 6 apples if they are average size). While the apples are cooking, mix the cobbler dough.

Use **1 cup flour, 1/4 teaspoon salt, 2 teaspoons baking powder, 3 tablespoons melted butter** and **1/3 cup milk.** Mix flour, baking powder and salt, add the milk and shortening and stir. This forms a soft dough which you roll out on a lightly floured bread board, into the same shape as the baking dish.

Pour the apples into a deep pan approximately 8" x 10" in size. Have enough juice to come to the top of the apples, and add ½ cup or more of sugar, depending on the tartness of the apples.

Sprinkle with **½ teaspoon cinnamon** or **¼ teaspoon nutmeg** or both if you like the combination, dot with **two or three tablespoons butter,** then cover with the dough. Cut the dough in squares with a sharp knife and bake at 425° for 20 minutes or until the dough is well browned.

This cobbler is good served hot, and you may choose from a variety of sauces.

Two cups of very rich milk, seasoned with **4 tablespoons sugar and ½ teaspoon fresh grated nutmeg,** is excellent.

A heaping **tablespoon of whipped cream** makes the cobbler a very special serving.

You may use the same sauce as used on bread pudding which adds flavor and piquancy to the dessert, or you may make a hard sauce.

HARD SAUCE

A hard sauce is easy to make.

Cream **1 cup powdered or confectioner's sugar** with **1/3 cup butter** until light and fluffy. Use either **1 teaspoon vanilla** or **lemon extract. Rum or brandy extract** gives a different flavor. **Two or 3 tablespoons orange juice** is also good, but if you use the orange juice, add a little more powdered sugar and beat until fluffy.

OTHER COBBLERS

The same amount of either fresh or canned peaches as apples, will make an excellent cobbler. The same cobbler crust is very suitable.

Blackberries also make a delicious cobbler. Use **3 or 4 cups of berries** and **juice, 1 cup sugar, 2 tablespoons butter,** but no spices. Use the **standard cobbler crust** and you really have a dessert that is mouth watering. A serving of **vanilla ice cream,** especially the home made kind, on the blackberry cobbler makes the family ask for another helping.

Both tame and wild plums may be used in cobblers. A palatable cobbler is made from rhubarb sauce.

Sometimes I cut the rolled dough with a biscuit cutter and place the biscuit on steaming hot fruit. At other times if I am in a big hurry, I add 3 or 4 tablespoons milk to thin the mixed dough and then drop by teaspoons on the fruit. The dough spreads out over the fruit and cooks to a crispy brown. It may not be as decorative as the biscuits, but just as good.

OLD MARTHA AND UNCLE GEORGE

One time Uncle Sid and Uncle Bert had been over on the flats on the Little Muddy and when they came back they brought a cat called Martha with them. The homesteaders didn't want her any more, so they sent Martha to Olive and me. What a cat!

We liked her in spite of her appearance. She was a decided calico with very distinct orange, brown, and black markings with white chest, stomach and legs. Her ears and tail had been frozen until they were much shorter than originally planned.

We dressed Martha in doll clothes and then we had to laugh. She looked so indignant and her diminished tail swung around angrily, but she seldom scratched us. We didn't know her age, but the old home-steader told the uncles that she was at least 9 or 10 years old. She probably was, as she was an old warrior — and she would take on gophers and weasels or any dog that came around. She got along fine with Jum, our shepherd dog, but that probably was out of necessity.

One summer, Uncle George Stites, Grandma's brother, came to visit us. Uncle George was tall, slender and dignified with a great deal of white hair and a white beard. Uncle George slept in the front room. We were all used to Martha — but Uncle George wasn't. Some nights Martha would climb to the roof of the shack, and tramp back and forth across the roof yowling. The volume of her yowling almost competed with the coyotes.

Uncle George couldn't sleep. No wonder, as the roof was made by a single layer of pine boards covered by tarpaper. After the second night of Martha's entertainment, Uncle George was quite tired. He didn't swear, but his remarks about what he thought of Martha and what he would like to do to her worried Olive and me. We caught Martha and fastened her in a box at the barn for the night. When we let her out the next morning, she angrily stalked away across the prairie, switching her stumpy tail. We didn't see her again for several days, but Uncle George got his rest.

Uncle George enjoyed Mamma's cooking — and he especially had a fondness for fresh corn boiled on the cob.

CORN ON THE COB

Husking the corn and removing the silk was a job that fell to Olive and me. The ears were big and sometimes we really worked hard to get the husks off. We pulled all silks off carefully. Mamma trimmed both ends of the ear with a butcher knife, then dropped the corn into a big kettle of boiling water. Boil tender corn for 10 minutes, and more mature corn for 15 to 20 minutes. To check the tenderness of corn, cut a kernel of corn with a finger nail. If it is quite milky, it is young and tender; if the milk is thick and congealed, the corn is more mature.

That corn was delicious as it came steaming hot from the kettle. We smeared some butter on the corn, sprinkled it with salt and pepper and started eating. Olive always sat by Uncle George, and they both would eat corn heartily. Olive tried to eat more than Uncle George, but she didn't do too well. Uncle George would divert Olive's attention then slip his empty cob onto the pile by her plate. She was very proud of all the corn she thought she had eaten.

WILTED LETTUCE

Uncle George also liked wilted lettuce. Mamma gathered the lettuce, being careful to pull it out carefully so no loose leaves would fall back on the remainder to make it spoil. She also thinned the lettuce as she gathered it.

Grandpa planted Hansen lettuce. It is not ordinarily thought of as a head lettuce, but will head-up to a loosely formed head if properly thinned.

Mamma did the cleaning and washing of the lettuce. She was afraid I might leave some bugs or little worms on the leaves. Mamma filled a big dishpan with lettuce. After it was washed she would drain it, take a big knife and cut criss-cross through the lettuce in the pan 6 to 8 times. Then she diced several green onions on top of the lettuce.

Mamma **fried several slices of bacon** in the big iron skillet which she put aside on a meat platter in a warm place. She poured off all but **4 or 5 tablespoons of bacon grease, added 1/3 cup vinegar** and **1/3 cup water** and **1/2 cup sugar** and **1/2 teaspoon salt** to the bacon grease and brought to a boil. Then she took the skillet from the heat and turned the lettuce into the dressing, stirred it well and poured it into a serving bowl. It is called wilted lettuce, and it is wilty, but is certainly good and tasty.

Corn on the cob, wilted lettuce, bacon and boiled potatoes with their jackets, buffalo berry jelly, and dried apple pie, was a hearty and mouth-watering meal.

Here is another method for making wilted lettuce. Sometimes after the dressing came to a boil, Mamma dropped in a couple of **slightly beaten eggs** and stirred until the eggs were all cooked into little chunks, then added the lettuce. I like this, too. I use only leaf lettuce for wilting.

DRIED CORN

After we had several meals of the tender sweet corn, Grandpa brought in a big tub full of corn to be husked, silked and boiled. Mamma boiled the corn for ten minutes, or just enough to set the milk in the kernels, and poured off the boiling water. Then she spread the ears on pans to cool. When cooled, Mamma took a sharp knife and cut off the kernels. The cut corn was put into sugar sacks, 2 or 3 pounds to a sack, tied securely and pinned on the clothes line. The hot sun began the drying process. Occasionally we went out and shook the sacks so the drying would be even. At night the corn would be taken in, for there might be an unexpected shower, or a heavy dew. It took several days to dry the corn completely so there was no danger of mildew or spoilage.

Sometimes we dried corn by spreading the kernels ½ inch thick in bread pans and placing in a warm oven. Today a 200° oven would be warm enough. If the oven was quite warm, we left the door slightly ajar and stirred quite often to prevent the corn sticking to the pan or scorching.

This method of drying corn is faster than drying by the sun. I like it better, as the corn is slightly browned and has a richer flavor. When stored in an airtight can, it will last two or three years and still be good.

CREAMED DRIED CORN

Dried corn is good creamed, in soup, and in chowder.

Soak **2 cups of corn** overnight in 6 cups of water. Simmer for two or three hours or until done. By this time the corn will have cooked almost dry. It may be necessary to add water during cooking time. Put in **2 tablespoons butter, ½ teaspoon salt, ¼ teaspoon black pepper** and **½ cup rich milk or cream.** It is good to add one cup instead of ½ cup milk or cream and use some thickener. This is really a tasty dish.

One-fourth cup diced onion and **¼ cup of diced pimento** gives a tang to creamed dried corn.

DRIED CORN SOUP

Dried corn soup makes a substantial meal, just by itself. Use the **same amount of corn as for creamed corn.** One hour or half-hour before corn is tender, **add 1 teaspoon salt, ¼ teaspoon pepper,** and **1 diced onion,** when the corn and onion is done, add **1 quart of milk** and **3 tablespoons of butter** and bring to the boiling point, then serve with either crackers or biscuits. A variation would be to add a **cup of diced raw bacon** to the corn while it is cooking or **crumbled fried bacon** just before serving.

CORN CHOWDER

Corn chowder is also very good made with dried corn. Soak **2 cups of dried corn** overnight and simmer until done. Add **2 medium size potatoes** and **2 small onions** either sliced or diced, about one-half hour before meal time. Just before serving, season with **1 teaspoon salt, ¼ teaspoon black pepper, a cup of crumbled fried bacon, 2 tablespoons bacon fryings** and **2 to 4 cups of milk,** (depending on personal preference) plus a **small amount of thickener.** Have some cold cabbage for your relish and a dried apple pie for dessert. This is a stick-to-the-ribs dinner.

CORN-OFF-THE-COB

Mamma sometimes cut the corn off the cob and boiled it in a small amount of water until done. When cooked, she added **salt** and **pepper** and **2 tablespoons butter,** or **2 tablespoons bacon fryings.** Although this was good, I really liked "corn on the cob" better.

CORN PUDDING

Another corn dish that was popular with the family was corn pudding. When the corn was past the tender stage, but not yet hard, Mamma took a sharp knife and just clipped off the tops of the kernels of corn, and then scraped the cob to get the thick milky portion of the kernel.

Use **2 to 3 cups of the cut corn, 3 beaten eggs, 2 cups milk, 1 tablespoon sugar, ½ teaspoon salt, and 1/8 teaspoon black pepper.** Mix thoroughly and pour into a greased baking dish 9"x9"x3" and cook at 350° for 1½ hours. When the pudding is done, it becomes firm and may be cut in squares.

You may also use the canned creamed corn in the same proportions. Corn pudding is served as a vegetable, not as a dessert.

CORN RELISH

Corn relish added variety to the menu served on the homestead, and is just as good today.

Use **5 cups fresh corn cut from the cob, ½ cup ground red sweet pepper and ½ cup ground green pepper, 2 cups diced celery, 1 cup diced onion, 1½ cups water, 1½ cups vinegar, 3 cups sugar, 2 oz. white mustard seed, 1 oz. celery seed, 1 teaspoon turmeric and 2 teaspoons salt.**

Cook this mixture at a slow boil for 30 minutes. Sometimes it is necessary to add more water so there will be sufficient liquid on the corn relish. When canned it should be quite moist but not runny. Can and seal in sterilized pint jars. It has an inviting look on the pantry shelf and is welcome at the table.

HOMINY

Hominy and hominy grits are not just foods of the deep south — they are used in southern Indiana. Of course, Tom Lincoln came into Indiana from Kentucky and some of the Romines came from Virginia. In the early days, each family took care of its own larder by producing and processing its own food and hunting its own meat.

Grandpa prepared corn for hominy in a large enamel pail.

You may make hominy from ripe sweet or field corn. **Shell the corn** and place in an iron or porcelain kettle. Use **2 quarts of water for every pint of corn. Add 2 rounded teaspoons of concentrated lye.** Bring to a boil and simmer for 20 to 30 minutes stirring often during the last part of the cooking. Remove from heat and allow to stand 15 to 20 minutes. Now wash thoroughly to remove excess lye. You may either rub vigorously by hand or place in a churn and churn several minutes.

It is necessary to churn or rub to remove the softened hulls and the black tips of the corn.

The hominy now stands several hours in water which is frequently changed. Or it may be "thrash" boiled; that is it may be boiled for a few minutes; the water poured off; more water added and boiled again. This process is repeated until no lye is left. Of course we had some hominy to eat right away, but the majority was dried and then stored for winter use.

It was either spread out in bread pans, covered with cheese cloth and set in the sun to dry, or put in cloth sugar sacks and tied to the clothes line where it dried for several days.

Cover **2 cups of dried hominy** with **5 cups of cold water** and soak all night. In the morning bring to a hard boil, reduce the heat to simmer until the hominy is tender. Check from time to time so the hominy will not boil dry. Season by adding **2 tablespoons of bacon or ham fryings, salt and pepper** and simmer for a few minutes before serving. Either fried ham or bacon is a suitable meat to serve with hominy.

Another method of making hominy is to use soda. A suggested amount is as follows: **Shell eight ears of corn** having very large kernels and put into an iron or enamel kettle. **Cover with water** and **add two tablespoons of baking soda.** Then follow the same process as used in the making of hominy by the lye solution.

A winter supply of hominy would necessitate more corn and the

amount of either the lye or soda, in proportion to the amount of corn.

I was amazed that Grandpa could take just plain corn and make hominy. He used the lye method.

DRYING PARSLEY

Across the end of the garden nearest the house was a row of parsley, twenty feet long and about a foot wide. Grandpa started it from seed and the second year it was a foot tall, a fluffy dark green waving in the winds. Olive and I loved to pick sprigs to chew on.

When the days grew long and hot, Grandpa would dry parsley. He built a box, approximately 30 inches square and three feet tall, with legs at each corner. The top and sides were covered with wire screen, and it had two wooden shelves.

He thoroughly washed the parsley, dried it, and then placed it in his drying box. He turned the parsley every day until it was powdery dry. Then he rolled it into very small flakes which he stored in airtight containers for winter. A shaker of flaked parsley always stood on the table with the salt and pepper. Grandpa used it on most of his foods.

I especially remember his shaking it over milk gravy that he had spooned over his buttermilk biscuits for breakfast.

"SALIMAGUNDI" — A SALAD THAT IS DIFFERENT

Aunt Ella found this Salimagundi recipe in a paper or magazine before the family migration to Montana.

Chop 2 cups tomatoes
1 cup celery
1 cup cucumbers
1 cup mango peppers into ¼ inch pieces

and **salt** until it has a slightly over-salted taste. Let stand for 5 to 6 hours or overnight. Drain and then squeeze out any remaining juice. Use the same basic dressing used for the slaw.

If you want an attractive salad, take a thick slice from the top of the tomato, scoop out the center of the tomato and make scallops around the top. Fill the hollow tomato with the prepared salad. The plate may have a green decoration of lettuce or parsley.

"Sali" or salimagundi makes an excellent salad. Be sure to have plenty because your family or guests will want seconds.

We did not have this salad for Christmas, though, for our country stores did not import tomatoes, cucumbers, or peppers in the winter, and for a long time only in limited quantities in the summer, but we did have celery.

The celery was considered edible only when bleached by covering it as it was maturing or even storing and bleaching. It was rather tasteless, I thought. The green celery today has more food value and is much more palatable.

FRIED FISH EGGS

I remember one summer when Uncle John, Aunt Flora, and their daughters, Helen and Olive, came to visit. When Uncle John's Olive was named they lived in North Dakota and we lived in Indiana and no complications were foreseen, but we also moved west and were together quite a little as we grew up.

This particular time, Grandpa and Uncle John went fishing in Medicine Lake, and caught several carp. That night, we had fish for supper. It was dark before supper was on the table. The only light was from a reflector wall-lamp and another lamp on the table. Even with those two lamps it was difficult to see the small fish bones, so the grownups decided that we girls could only have the fried fish eggs because it would be difficult to get all the fish bones out.

So we sat eating fried fish eggs and the grownups ate those beautiful, crisp brown fish.

Masses of fish eggs found in a 9 to 12 inch fish are small orange objects much the size of the head of a pin. The masses of eggs are held together by tissue filaments and when **salted, peppered, dipped in corn meal** and fried a crisp brown are about the size of a hen egg. I think they have a decidedly flat taste.

Some fishermen behead the fish when caught, split full length underneath from the gills to tail and remove the entrails. Other fishermen just throw the fish into a bag and bring them home to clean. Here, they will be beheaded by removing the head above the gills. The next steps are cutting off the fins and tail, removing the scales by scraping with a knife from the tail toward the head, slitting open the belly full length of the fish, and removing the entrails.

The fish has an air sack inside which looks somewhat like an elongated balloon about the size of the thumb. The size depends, of course, on the size of the fish.

The small "balloon" when dried was fun to play with, and sometimes we had several of these miniature balloons.

FRIED FISH

The fish may either be split in half length ways, or split so they will lie flat in a skillet. Sprinkle with **salt**, dip in **yellow corn meal**, and fry in plenty of **hot shortening — 6 to 8 tablespoons bacon drippings or lard —** to a crunchy brown.

Fish can be served with fresh fried potatoes, green onions, green beans (warmed over from the noon meal) sliced cucumbers, hot biscuits and apple pie — plus the fried fish eggs!

WATERMELON PICKLES AND PRESERVES

I remember a big shade tree in the back yard at Grandpa's home in

Indiana. A long grape arbor was on the left side of the tree, and there was a long picnic table under the tree. The family would gather here sometimes on hot afternoons to eat cool, refreshing watermelon, which had been cooled by ice blocks cut from the ice pond and stored between layers of sawdust. This ice lasted all summer and was used as a cooling agent when needed and for making ice cream.

Those huge watermelons were cool, luscious and sweet, and we ate all we wanted. Grandpa sometimes cut two or three and we ate only the best parts. The rest was thrown to the hogs.

Occasionally we made watermelon preserves and pickles from the rind. The rind includes the green peel and the white meat.

In Montana, after the first year or two, watermelons were shipped in from the south and middle states. On the homestead, watermelons did not ripen well, but Uncle Sid grew beautiful big melons when he moved down from Canada and homesteaded in the red hills near Sarpy Creek. When we had watermelons, Mamma would save the rind, if it was thick, for pickles and preserves.

Peel off all the green part and trim away any pink that might be left on the thick white part of the rinds. **Dice the white portion into ½ inch chunks.** Soak overnight in a mild salt solution — **½ cup salt to 1 gallon of water.** Drain and put **12 cups watermelon rind,** into a syrup made of **10 cups of sugar, 8 cups of water,** the **juice of 3 medium-size lemons,** a spice bag with **2 teaspoons crushed stick cinnamon and 2 teaspoons cloves.** Bring to a boil and simmer until tender and transparent. Can and seal in sterilized pint jars. The cooking process will take around an hour.

Watermelon rind may also be pickled. Use **12 cups of the diced rind, 10 cups of sugar, 4 cups vinegar and 4 cups of water.** Place **4 teaspoons crushed stick cinnamon, 2 teaspoons whole cloves,** and **1 teaspoon mustard seed** in a spice bag and drop into the mixture.

Bring the watermelon to a boil and simmer until transparent and can in sterilized jars.

SPICE BAG

If you do not have a small cotton sack, take a five or six inch square of light weight white cotton material. Pile the spices in the center of the cloth, pull corners together. Pull a strong cord around the cloth, so none of the spices may fall out.

CITRON PRESERVES AND PICKLES

Aunt Ella raised her own citron and made citron preserves and pickles. A citron is shaped much like a watermelon, but as a rule is not nearly as big. The centers are pale apple green, almost white. The citron is not eaten raw, but practically all may be used for canning, except for the outer peeling. The same process used in making watermelon preserves or pickles may be used in making citron preserves and pickles. They are tasty and give variety to the foods stored for winter usage.

Candied citron is, now as then, found in grocery stores and is used in fruit cakes and plum puddings.

BOILED CABBAGE

Mamma quite often boiled cabbage with potatoes. She cut a **medium size head** into eighths, cutting through the core so the cabbage leaves were held together. She used a large kettle and put **6 or 8 quartered and peeled potatoes** in the bottom of the kettle, and then lay the cabbage on top. She spread a thin layer of **bacon grease** over the cabbage, then sprinkled with **salt** and **pepper**. She poured in **two cups of hot water,** brought to a boil, and set the kettle on the back of the stove to simmer for one-half hour. The bacon fryings seeped down through the cabbage, seasoning both the cabbage and potatoes. **Butter** instead of bacon fryings spread on the cabbage also made a good seasoning.

Cabbage and potatoes made a good dinner served with fried or baked ham, and a pan of corn bread.

SWEET-SOUR STEWED CABBAGE

Chop a **quart of cabbage** into inch pieces and simmer in a 3 quart kettle with **1/2 cup of water, 2 tablespoons butter, 2 tablespoons vinegar, 2 to 3 tablespoons sugar, 1/2 teaspoon salt, 1/8 teaspoon pepper,** and simmer until tender. When tender, add a **scant teaspoon of soda,** stir. Just before serving, pour in **1/4 cup of cream.**

We liked this type of cooked cabbage very much, but seldom served it to guests because the cream might curdle. It was only by experimenting that we came up with the soda idea and it works beautifully.

I call this a sweet-sour stewed cabbage. Mamma just called it vinegar cabbage; I think we must have acquired the present name because the Chinese sweet-sour foods have been well publicized.

HOT CABBAGE

Mamma could almost make a meal on hot cabbage. She would begin with **4 cups finely chopped cabbage, one small finely chopped onion,** (if available) **one chopped green sweet pepper, one chopped red sweet pepper, and one small red hot pepper.** Then she would make a cold dressing of ¼ cup vinegar, ¼ cup of water, 4 tablespoons of sugar, 1 teaspoon salt and ¼ teaspoon of black pepper. These were mixed well and allowed to stand one hour before serving.

Mamma enjoyed hot cabbage with hot biscuits, plenty of butter and perhaps fried ham or bacon. Either boiled potatoes in the jacket or fried potatoes helped to prevent the burn of the hot peppers in the cabbage.

If you are a "red" pepper person, you will enjoy this dish. I am not a "red" pepper person.

TURNIPS AND RUTABAGAS

Grandpa raised turnips and rutabagas in his garden. Both of these vegetables are very good when eaten raw. Pull, wash, and peel a turnip or rutabaga, then either slice and eat or eat as you sometimes eat an apple, taking a bite from the sweet crunchy vegetable. A sprinkle of salt is good.

Wash, **peel and slice 8 cups of turnips.** Use **2 cups of water** and just maintain enough water so the turnips will not boil dry. Keep covered while cooking and stew until tender. Add **2 to 3 tablespoons butter, 1 teaspoon salt,** and **½ teaspoon of black pepper.** Another way to season this vegetable is to cook and cream by adding **1 cup of milk and some thickener.** Simmer until the milk thickens. Add **butter to taste.**

Cook rutabagas in the same way. One time a friend who was very fond of rutabagas had supper with us and after eating creamed rutabagas declared that they were divine. Creamed rutabagas really are good, but I personally would never go so far as to say they are divine.

It seems to me that a well browned slice of ham, hot corn bread and

sorghum, and some mango pickles are good table mates for either turnips and rutabagas.

The tops of both the turnips and rutabagas are good when cooked as greens.

TURNIP SLAW

If by chance you want a dish of cole slaw and have no cabbage, but do have **turnips or rutabagas,** grate enough to fill **4 cups.** Make the basic cooked vinegar dressing and pour over the grated turnips or rutabagas. Season with **salt and pepper** for an excellent salad.

MANGO PEPPERS

Early freezes sometimes killed the pepper plants, but when Mamma was able to obtain the Mango peppers (large green or red bell shaped peppers) either from the garden or the store, she made pickled mangos.

Wash the peppers thoroughly. Cut off the top with a sharp knife, and remove the seeds and core. **Soak the peppers** over night in a **strong brine,** made by putting sufficient salt into the water to give it a very salty taste.

The next morning drain off the brine. **Chop or grate cabbage and salt lightly.** Fill the peppers tightly with the cabbage. A **small diced onion and diced green and red peppers** are also good when mixed in the chopped cabbage.

Cover each quart of peppers with a **pickling solution made of one cup vinegar and 1 cup sugar.** Boil and pour hot over the peppers. The peppers may be packed in quart jars or in a 2 gallon stone jar. If more liquid is needed add enough boiling water to fill the jar.

Mamma made it this way and it is good, but I like it better when I use ¼ **cup water** and ¾ **cup vinegar.** You may triple or quadruple this amount to cover the gallon of peppers. If you pack in a big jar, place an inverted plate over the peppers, weight down with a smooth rock and cover the jar with a cloth and heavy lid. Let stand in a cool place. The mangos will be ready to serve in three weeks. If you pack in quart jars, follow the usual canning procedure.

These peppers are a very fine relish to serve with roasts, or fried meats. If both red peppers and green peppers are pickled, they make a very decorative center dish.

When selecting peppers, use the small ones as the large ones make a very big serving and may have to be halved or quartered.

They may also be put in wide mouth quart or half-gallon glass jars and sealed after the hot vinegar solution is added and seal according to the directions of the jar manufacturer.

Remember, we sometimes get very strong vinegar. In that case, use ¼ cup of water to ¾ cups of vinegar or even half. You may have to reduce the strength even more. I sometimes use half water and half vinegar.

The cabbage works and forms a certain amount of gas pressure, so if the jars are sealed, liquid may "spew" out, but after the cabbage is through working, the jars will reseal. Check occasionally, though, to see if they are sealed.

CUCUMBERS, HOMESTEAD STYLE

Grandpa always raised many cucumbers, so we had all the fresh cucumbers and pickles we wanted.

Olive and I liked to take 4 and 5 inch young tender cucumbers right from the patch, peel and eat them with a little salt.

We relished their sweet tenderness. Mamma would serve sliced cucumbers for dinner or supper. Once in a while she would slice a **quart of cucumbers,** add a **cup of vinegar** and a **cup of water,** a **cup of sugar,** and a **tablespoon of salt,** and let stand overnight. Sometimes she would add **two or three sliced onions** to these cucumber slices, and the combination makes a zesty relish with meat.

We had fresh sweet pickles early in cucumber season.

Without peeling, slice a **quart of cucumbers** and soak overnight in a **mild salt solution** (slightly more salty than you like your foods). The next morning pour off the salty water, simmer gently for a minute in **1 cup vinegar, 1 to 2 cups water, 1 cup sugar,** and ¼ **teaspoon of black pepper.**

This makes a very good quick pickle to use as a relish with the fall foods. I like to eat these pickles with cold biscuits for snacks.

FRIED CUCUMBERS

Occasionally, when the cucumbers grew very large and started to turn yellow, they were fried. Wash and slice the **cucumber ¼ inch thick lengthways.** Dip the slices into **salted, slightly beaten eggs** then dip into **flour** and fry in **medium hot grease** a crispy brown. They are really good and were the homesteaders' answer to a yen for eggplant.

Fry slices of large green tomatoes in the same manner — you will be surprised how good they taste.

PICKLES IN BRINE

The big, wooden pickle barrel stood covered in the back hall, more than half filled with a strong salt brine. The brine was made of water and mixed with enough salt so a fresh egg floated in it. The pickle barrel seemed very large to me. It must have been nearly 3 feet tall with a diameter of 18 to 20 inches or more.

As cucumbers were brought in from the garden, they were washed, stemmed and dropped into the brine. A big platter placed over the cucumbers, weighed down with a stone, kept them covered with the brine. The barrel was covered with an old blanket or a lid.

During the winter if Mamma wanted pickles, she would take several cucumbers from the brine, and freshen them by soaking in clear water for a couple of days, changing the water several times. These cucumbers would either be sliced or pickled whole.

For **four quarts of pickles** make a pickling solution with **2½ cups vinegar, 2½ cups water, 4 cups sugar** and bring to a boil. Put **4 teaspoons celery seed,** and **2 tablespoons mustard** into a small cloth bag, fasten the top, and drop into boiling liquid and boil 5 minutes. Add the freshened cucumber and bring to boiling point, but *do not* boil. Store in a stone jar.

It has been my experience dry land cucumbers are better for this method of making pickles. They seem to remain firm longer. The altitude is also responsible for variations in pickle making.

ANOTHER FUN DAY – MAKING SAUERKRAUT

Grandpa and Mamma made a big 10 gallon jar of kraut in the late fall. Mamma trimmed all the outside leaves from the cabbage, and then Grandpa and Mamma took turns cutting the cabbage on an old kraut cutter that had been Grandma's. They put the cutting board across a big dish pan and they rubbed cabbage across the knives. The finely cut shreds fell in the pan.

Each time the dishpan became full, the **cabbage** was dumped into a 100 pound flour sack that had been placed in the big brown jar. Grandpa added **2 tablespoons salt,** then bruised and kneaded the shredded cabbage until it was limp and watery. Finally, the jar was nearly filled with the cabbage. Then Grandpa mixed and bruised all the cabbage in the big jar. When he tasted the cabbage – Olive and I tasted, too. If Grandpa decided there was not enough salt, he kept adding some salt, mixing and tasting until the cabbage was too salty for table use, but it was still edible.

By now the salty juices practically covered the cabbage. Grandpa twisted the top of the sack down tightly, then placed a large clean cloth entirely over the sack. He turned a big plate over the cloth, weighing down the plate with a 4 or 5 pound smooth rock. The pressure of the rock brought the liquid up above the plate.

If you follow this procedure, place the jar in a cool dark place for the cabbage to work and become sauerkraut. If the cabbage is very firm and dry, there might not be enough juice. In that case stir enough water into the cabbage to come slightly above the kraut. This seldom happens, but it does occasionally. Also the amount of juice will vary with the humidity in the atmosphere. If it is a very dry fall, it may also be necessary to add water later. The kraut should be ready by the time the pigs are butchered, or in five or six weeks.

Remove the rock and plate from the jar, then remove the cloth carefully so that you get all scum that may have formed. Open the big sack. If the top layer is soft, take it out and throw away, then take out a kettle of the firm sweet kraut. The raw kraut is very delicious to eat, just as it comes from the jar.

SAUERKRAUT AND SPARE RIBS

Grease a big bread pan and put in a layer of the **spare ribs,** add a **sprinkling of salt and pepper,** then add another layer of spare ribs and seasoning. Place in a hot oven. As the ribs bake, turn occasionally so that they are well browned. They will be ready to serve in approximately one hour.

In the meanwhile, add a little water to the kraut and simmer slowly on the back of the stove. As the ribs bake, fat will drip into the pan. Some of this **fat** may be used to **season the kraut.** Boil a **kettle of potatoes** in their jackets, and at the table **season with butter, salt, and pepper.** A dish of sliced onions seasoned with salt, pepper, sugar and half water and half vinegar dressing makes a good relish for the ribs, sauerkraut and potatoes.

Add to this menu a pan of corn bread, both as a bread and as a dessert with sorghum or honey.

CORN BREAD

Stir in mixing bowl **1½ cups yellow corn meal, 1½ cups flour, ½ teaspoon salt, 6 teaspoons baking powder, ½ teaspoon soda.** Beat in **2 eggs** with a few strokes of a fork, pour in **1½ cups buttermilk,** and add **¼ cup melted shortening.** Beat the entire mixture well and pour into two well-greased pound bread pans. It will take 20 to 25 minutes to bake to a deep brown in a 425° oven.

SAUERKRAUT TODAY

When I make kraut today, I place the **shredded and bruised cabbage** immediately into a quart jar. I pack it very firmly to within ¾ inches of the top and add ¾ **teaspoon of salt and 1 scant teaspoon sugar.** The juice from the cabbage should come within ½ inch of the top of the jar. If there is not sufficient liquid, pour in a little water, running a knife blade down between the jar and the cabbage to allow this moisture to seep down. When there is sufficient moisture, cover tightly with a sterilized lid.

Place this canned kraut in a dark cool place to work. As it works some juice may spew out, so have several layers of paper on the shelf to catch the moisture.

When the kraut quits working, the jars will seal. Check the kraut occasionally for once in a great while, it may darken at the top. If any does, use that jar right away, or put in the refrigerator until needed.

I seldom have any spoilage with this method, and I have an excellent sauerkraut. If you use this method and have refrigerator space, store in the refrigerator, after the kraut has finished working.

NEXT CAME FALL

After the fall rains came the long lazy days of Indian summer.

Wheat stood in tall shocks waiting for the threshing crews. The grasses turned yellow, then brown. The wide blue western sky gradually blended to shades of orange and red that followed the setting sun. That brilliance also faded into the night, with the incessant drone of insects, stilling.

The occasional lonesome howl of a coyote, answered by another and another from around the prairie's perimeter echoed through the hushed night.

BUFFALO BERRIES AND CHOKE CHERRIES

Occasionally in late August, but usually in September, and sometimes even as late as October, the choke cherries would ripen. After a frost, the buffalo berries would be ready to pick.

Jo and Dick would be hitched to the wagon, big buckets and tubs would be loaded and Mamma, and the relatives would go berrying.

Sometimes Olive and I would get to go, but generally we stayed home with Grandpa. They hunted the berries in the brakes along the Little Muddy and over in the sand hills. If Olive and I went, we had to stay near the wagon, and we picked berries on the lower bushes. We weren't allowed to go running around over the hills. Mamma was afraid we might get lost. Also, there were adders and rattlesnakes in the sand hills, and that could be dangerous.

We liked to go though, as it was fun just to be along for the picnic lunch and to eat the berries fresh from the bush.

Choke cherries are rightly named – they seem to choke a person. The ripe berries were almost as large as peas, and black with big hard seeds. They were sweet, when ripe, but had a strong, tangy taste somewhat resembling a pie cherry. We were allowed to eat all we wanted, for we never did eat many. Our lips, our tongue, our teeth, and our hands became a dark, dark purple and soon our throats would become very dry, and scratchy. A sensation of choking followed and tears came into our eyes. A drink of water or a piece of bread helped, but as soon as we ate a few more berries, the choking started again.

We were never allowed to go when they went for buffalo berries. They grew on tall spreading bushes with silvery gray green leaves. The berries were small and protected by thorns, one or two inches long. They were very difficult to pick, but usually after a sharp frost the bushes could be shaken or beaten and the berries would shower down onto an old sheet or a canvas placed on the ground under the bushes. Why the buffalo would eat those berries I do not know. Perhaps their thick, shaggy hides protected them from the sharp thorns.

BUFFALO BERRY JELLY

The small, bright red berries make delicious jelly. They have to be washed and picked over very soon as they will become sticky and cling together in big clusters.

Cover the **berries** with **water** and boil several minutes. Strain the juice through two or three layers of cheese cloth, then measure it back into a big kettle. Add the **same number of cups of sugar** as you have juice. Stir and boil until double drops fall from the side of the spoon, then pour into sterilized glasses and jars. Buffalo berries make beautiful jelly, a clear light orange with a red cast. It can be used in place of cranberries with meat or chicken.

Evidently, the buffalo berry has a great deal of pectin as it jells very easily, and the berries can be covered with water a second time, boiled again, and another batch of jelly made. Of course, this is a lighter orange, but still has a delicious flavor.

BUFFALO BERRY CATSUP

Violet experimented with the buffalo berries and made an excellent catsup. In reality, you make buffalo berry catsup much as you make tomato catsup. When I buy tomato catsup, I buy by brand name as different companies make a different flavored catsup. I like foods that are not highly seasoned, so adjust the following recipe according to the likes or dislikes of your family.

Cook a large kettle of buffalo berries, using just enough water to come to the top of the berries. Simmer until the berries are mushy, allow to cool and put through a colander. The berries have many small seeds, so there will not be very much pulp.

Use a **gallon of the juice and pulp**, add to this **two large diced onions** and cook until the onions are done, and put through the colander. If you do not want to bother with the fresh onions, use two or three teaspoons of powdered onion. Use **3 cups vinegar** (4 cups if you like a sour catsup) **4 cups sugar, 2 teaspoons cinnamon, ½ teaspoon cloves, and ½ teaspoon of allspice.**

Simmer until the juice has the consistency of tomato catsup, stirring often to prevent scorching. Can in sterilized glass jars.

Note: Since the buffalo berries are very tart, you may wish to use one less cup of vinegar, or add an additional cup of sugar.

CHOKE CHERRY JELLY

I like the choke cherries better than the buffalo berries.

Wash the cherries, removing any bugs, worms, or spoiled berries, cover with water and boil several minutes until the skins crack open. The juice will color the water a dark purple. Drain the juice from the berries, and work the pulp from the cherry seeds by rubbing through a colander.

Another method of obtaining the pulp is to put the cherries into a strong cloth sugar sack, twist the top very tightly and press and pound until the purple pulp comes slowly squeezing out. This operation is very detrimental to hand care and the purple stain may last for several days.

Choke cherry juice evidently has little pectin as Mamma could seldom make it jell without apple juice. After combining **equal amounts of choke cherry and apple juice, add sugar, cup for cup, with the juice.** Boil until the syrup falls from the edge of the spoon in double drops, then pour into sterilized and heated jelly glasses. Cover jelly with hot paraffin.

CHOKE CHERRY JAM

Mamma would also make choke cherry-apple jam by combining the **pulp of the cherries with an equal amount of unsweetened apple sauce.** Measure an **equal amount of sugar** into the fruit mixture and cook until double drops fall from the edge of the spoon. Put in jars and cover with paraffin and after it cools put on the lids.

CHOKE CHERRY SYRUP

These jellies and jams are very good, but what I really like is choke cherry syrup. To the **juice and pulp, add 3/4 the amount of sugar** and boil until thick and bubbly. The syrup may be canned like any fruit and will keep indefinitely. The children and grandchildren feel that they are having a special treat if I serve them hot biscuits, or pancakes, or waffles and choke cherry syrup. (They probably would have made good homesteaders!)

A hot buttermilk biscuit, butter and choke cherry jelly plus a hot cup of coffee makes a delightful snack. I go next door and share this treat with my young neighbor. She likes my old fashioned cooking.

CHOKE CHERRY JELLY TODAY

I do make choke cherry jelly today. I use a combination of juice and pulp and one of the pectins on the market, according to the directions given. They do not always give directions for choke cherries but they do for wild cherries and that works just as well. Wild cherries are very similar to choke cherries, only they seem to be slightly sweeter and perhaps just a little larger. I enjoy using either one in syrups, jams, and jellies, and I'm disappointed if I am not able to go choke cherrying every fall.

BLANC MANGE

Blanc mange is a very easy dessert to make. Olive and I learned to make it, and sometimes, Mamma would allow us to make it either for dessert or for between meal snacks. It is cheap but tasty and wholesome.

Thoroughly mix **3 tablespoons corn starch** and **3 tablespoons sugar.** Stir into this mixture **¼ cup cold milk.** Bring **1¾ cups milk** over slow heat to boiling point, and pour in the corn starch, sugar, milk mixture, stirring constantly to prevent sticking to the kettle and scorching. Continue stirring until thick. Flavor with **one scant teaspoon vanilla extract.**

When thick, pour into individual dessert dishes and put a **teaspoon of bright jelly** on center top. Blanc mange is also delicious served with rich milk or cream.

Blanc mange becomes a very good boiled custard if you use 2 tablespoons instead of 3 of the corn starch and when nearly done, add one well beaten egg to the mixture. Another serving suggestion would be to pour the blanc mange when cooled over fresh strawberries or fresh peaches. Serve with rich milk or cream.

We always cooked blanc mange in a kettle over direct heat in homestead days. I prefer cooking this type of food in the double boiler since it burns very easily over direct heat.

FLOAT OR FLOATING ISLAND

Float was a special dessert treat that we always enjoyed. Mamma was a versatile cook and knew how to prepare so many interesting foods.

This floating island recipe will make 6 to 8 generous servings. Mix **2 tablespoons corn starch** or **4 tablespoons flour** with **½ cup sugar** in a 4 quart kettle and mix with **½ cup cold milk.** Stir in **6 well beaten egg yolks.** Add **3½ cups heated milk** and stirring constantly cook over low heat until quite thick. Remove from heat and flavor with **1½ teaspoons vanilla extract.**

Put **¼ teaspoon salt** into the **egg whites** and beat until very fluffy. Add **6 tablespoons sugar,** one at a time, beating until the meringue is very stiff and glossy. Pour the egg whites into the cooked mixture; gently fold in 4 or 5 times so that chunks of meringue are not visible. Allow this hot dessert to stand for several minutes to finish cooking the meringue; then spoon into dessert dishes. **Fresh strawberries** make a piquant and attractive topping to the creamy texture and creamy color of the floating island.

PUMPKIN OR CARROT PIE

Mamma made delicious pumpkin pies or carrot pies in addition to the mince meat pies for Thanksgiving dinner. She used the same recipe for the pies (pumpkin or carrot) and we liked either one. The pumpkin pie had a smoother texture than the carrot pie, but they tasted much the same.

Today, you make a carrot pie with a fairly smooth texture by putting either cooked or raw carrots through a blender.

The following recipe makes either a good pumpkin or carrot pie.

To **1½ cups of mashed pumpkin or carrots** add ¾ cup brown sugar, **3 eggs beaten** with 20 strokes or more of a fork, **2 cups of rich milk or light cream, 1 teaspoon of cinnamon** and ½ teaspoon of nutmeg. Mix these ingredients well and pour into an uncooked pie shell. Bake at 425° for 15 minutes and lower heat to 350° and bake for 45 minutes or until a knife inserted in the center comes out clean.

When I was small it was such a temptation when those wonderful carrot and pumpkin pies were cooling. I wanted a taste so badly, I could hardly resist taking just a small spoonful of that custardy pumpkin or carrot. If Mamma made too much mixture, she would cook it in a small pan for Olive and me. That helped tide us over until mealtime.

PRUNE PIE

Since fresh fruits were not always available on the homestead, prune pie was often made. (We could always buy prunes.)

Stew one pound of prunes until very tender. Remove the seeds. Use **3 cups of prunes and juice,** (mostly prunes). To the prunes, add ½ **cup sugar, 3 tablespoons flour, 2 tablespoons lemon juice or vinegar,** and **one teaspoon cinnamon** or nutmeg. Use a **top crust.** Bake in a 425° oven for 10 minutes, then turn down the heat to 375° and bake for 40 minutes.

Another pie to add to my pie list is custard. There are custard pies and custard pies. Some are practically unedible, and some are very good.

The following recipe makes a very good custard pie.

CUSTARD PIE

Beat **3 eggs** with 50 strokes of a fork — add **¼ cup sugar** well mixed with **¼ teaspoon of salt**, stir in **2 cups of milk**, and **1 teaspoon of vanilla**. Bake in a 9-inch buttered **uncooked pie shell**. Sprinkle **grated nutmeg** over the top. Cook at 400° for 10 minutes and reduce the heat to 350° and cook for 30 minutes. If a knife comes clean when inserted in the center, the pie is done. Some good cooks bake a custard pie for 40 minutes at 425°. It works for them.

BAKED CUSTARD

Baked custard also is an excellent dessert.

Use **4 cups of scalded milk** and add **6 eggs** beaten with 50 strokes of the fork, **1/3 cup sugar**, **1/4 teaspoon salt**, **1 teaspoon vanilla extract**. After pouring into a slightly greased deep baking dish (5" x 9" x 3") sprinkle with **grated nutmeg**. Bake at 350° for 1 hour or until a knife inserted in the center comes clean. Put the custard dish in a pan of hot water while baking.

Check the custards very carefully, and remove immediately when done. An overcooked custard may be slightly watery.

CHESS PIE

(Set oven at 425° to pre-heat 10 to 15 minutes before placing pie in oven.)

Chess pie is a very rich and toothsome dessert. Mamma only made it occasionally, but it was a pie not to be forgotten and as far as taste is concerned was a favorite with me. In looking over old recipes, I find that Mamma got this particular recipe from Aunt Ella. The pie is a semi-custard but the texture is heavier, but richer.

The following is the filling for an eight inch pie. Put **1½ cups of sugar, 1 tablespoon plus 2 teaspoons of flour** into a medium size mixing bowl and stir well. Thoroughly work in **3½ tablespoons of butter**, then add **1 cup of rich milk or cream.** Add the **slightly beaten yolks of 3 eggs**, keeping the whites for the meringue. Flavor with **1 teaspoon vanilla extract.** Beat until smooth. Bake in a **single crust eight inch pie pan.** Grease the crust before pouring in the mixture. This keeps the bottom crust from becoming soggy.

Bake at 425° for 40 minutes. If the crust is getting too brown, lay a piece of aluminum foil over the pie, and another one below the pie pan. Test for doneness by inserting a knife blade into the filling. If the knife blade comes out clean, the pie is done.

When done, place pie pan on cooling rack, turn the oven down to 350° and make the meringue.

MERINGUE

Beat the **whites of the 3 eggs** until stiff, **add 6 tablespoons of sugar,** one at a time, beating after each addition. The meringue will now be stiff, will stand in peaks, and have a satiny look.

Pile the meringue on the pie, make swirly designs with the spoon and place the pie back into the oven and cook for 12 to 15 minutes. Watch carefully as meringue scorches easily. Bake only until entire surface is a soft brown. When cooling meringue, do not expose to drafts, as it might become beaded with small drops of moisture.

This pie could be cut into eight pieces instead of the traditional six, as it is very rich, very delicious, but heavily laden with calories.

HAVE A PIECE OF VINEGAR PIE!
(It's Good!)

My husband, Malcolm, is the son of prairie homesteaders, and I have heard so many times about the wonderful VINEGAR PIE that his mother used to make. Over the years, I have found various vinegar pie recipes which I have tried, but they were never "quite as good as mother used to make." I finally found my solution. Just make a lemon meringue pie, and instead of using lemon juice, add 2 tablespoons vinegar. I sometimes use a wine vinegar which is milder and gets away from the sharp acid taste. My husband admits that I finally made a good vinegar pie.

My guess is Malcolm's mother didn't have any lemon juice one time and just substituted vinegar for the juice, and it went over big with a family having three boys and one girl and so became a family tradition.

Here is the recipe that was finally accepted as good.

Mix until smooth **1½ cups sugar, 9 tablespoons flour, 1/8 teaspoon salt,** in the top of a 1½ to 2 quart double boiler. Add **1½ cups water,** cook until thick, stirring constantly. **Beat 3 egg yolks** twenty strokes with a fork, and add to cooked mixture. Mix well and cook until very thick. Remove from heat, add **2 tablespoons butter** and **2 tablespoons vinegar.** Cool.

Have the oven pre-heated to 350° and add the meringue that has been made from the 3 egg whites, using same directions as for Chess pie and bake 12 to 15 minutes.

SUGGESTIONS — Use 1 tablespoon vinegar and substitute 1 teaspoon lemon extract for 1 tablespoon vinegar.

        — Two tablespoons wine vinegar is good and not as acid as regular vinegar.

        — Always watch meringue, because it browns and burns very easily.

        — Mark the hot meringue with a sharp knife to prevent tearing when cutting the pie at serving time.

"MAMMA HOLLERED THE POTATOES OUT"

One cold windy day in late fall, Mamma decided to plow out the potatoes. She used a walking plow and Joe, our all-purpose horse. Joe had come to Montana in the boxcar and was part thoroughbred. He was in reality a saddle horse, but pulled a buggy, and did light work as a team with Dick.

Mamma would start down a row with the point of the plow share stuck under the first hill of potatoes. In holding the handles of the plow and trying to keep the share in the ground, she had difficulty with the lines. If she tilted the left handle of the plow, she also pulled on the left line — and Joe would turn left out of the nice straight potato row. Then she would start all over again. She would yell "Gee," "Haw" and "Whoa" and "Back-up." Joe would "Gee," "Haw," "Whoa" and "Back-up," but with Mamma trying to drag the plow into place and the wind swirling and blowing dirt around, things became more and more confused.

Finally Mamma put me on Joe's back to guide him. That didn't help matters any. I tried to keep him going straight down a row, but the plow share might hit a rock and bounce out or the share point go too deep — the plow had to be pulled back and Joe backed up and started all over again. Mamma would holler over the wind telling me what to

do, but she also had the lines, and we didn't always pull together. By this time, Joe was very confused. Besides, he didn't want to step on the potato tops or Russian thistles, so he went weaving around the plants.

Mamma was worn out trying to hold the plow share in the ground. She would holler at Joe — then she would holler at me. The cold wind puffed dirt into my face and eyes. Tears made streaked patches of mud down my cheeks.

But finally the plowing was done. We picked up those potatoes that were on top of the ground and the next day grubbed through the plowed dirt for those that were covered.

Mamma always laughed about "Hollering the potatoes out," when she told the story — but at the time, it certainly was no laughing matter. I still don't entirely appreciate the funny side of "Hollering the Potatoes Out."

Mamma stored several bushels of potatoes in the cellar for use until the next potato crop was harvested.

FOOD VALUE OF POTATOES

Potatoes were a staple food for our family and other families on the prairies. Many ate potatoes three times a day — fried for breakfast, boiled for dinner, warmed up for supper.

At the present time, potatoes are in ill-repute because they are thought of as a fattening food. In reality, they are only a fattener when too richly seasoned.

Before the food specialists analyzed the potato, some people realized that it held an important place in our diet. In early days, sailors did not get scurvy when away from land for long periods of time if they had potatoes to eat. Also, it is known that trappers and gold hunters in the far north did not have this dread disease if they had potatoes in their diet.

I found the following information in regard to the nutritive value of a medium size common potato in Bulletin No. 72 of the United States Department of Agriculture and the National Potato Council.

A medium size potato or 2/3 cups cooked potato has 30 percent of the daily requirements of vitamin C. It has only 90 calories. It contains calcium, protein, iron, phosphorus, potassium, vitamin B-1 and vitamin B-2 in sufficient quantities to be of value in any health program.

Potatoes are not as expensive as many foods, are easy to prepare and are a tasty addition to the day's menus.

POTATO SOUP WITH EGG DUMPLINGS

One soup that was easy to make and that we often had was potato soup with egg dumplings. It was a nutritious and substantial soup and was enough for a meal in itself.

The recipe I give is the one I use today. Use a **quart of raw potatoes** sliced ¼ inch thick; **one medium-size onion**, diced; **4 tablespoons butter; 1 quart water; 1 teaspoon salt**, and ¼ **teaspoon pepper**. Cook until the potatoes are almost tender. I use my 6 quart pressure cooker and follow the directions put out by the factory.

EGG DUMPLINGS

I now put the egg dumplings into the boiling mixture. To make the dumplings, break **2 medium or 1 large egg** into a small mixing bowl and beat 20 strokes with a fork. Add one generous **cup unsifted flour** and ¼ **teaspoon salt** to the beaten eggs and mix. If the eggs are very large, more flour may be needed. This forms a very stiff batter. Using the tip of the fork, take pieces of the batter about the size of a dime, drop into the boiling mixture, then swish the fork through the boiling soup. The next dumpling falls more easily because the fork is hot and moist.

Dropping in the dumplings is a rather tedious job, but do not become discouraged and put in large chunks of dough in order to hurry the process. The larger dumplings do not absorb the seasoning from the soup and simply are not as good as the smaller ones.

When all the dough has been dropped into the soup, cover the kettle, turn down the heat and simmer for 10 minutes. Break a dumpling open and if it is not sticky on the inside, the dumplings are done. If they are not done, cook a few minutes longer. The dumplings have no baking powder, but they do swell in the hot liquid.

After simmering 10 to 12 minutes, add a **can of evaporated milk** and bring to a boil and remove from heat. If you are lucky enough to have inherited an old fashioned soup bowl or tureen, fill it with the piping hot potato soup with tiny islands of those delectable yellow egg dumplings. Give it the place of honor in the middle of the table.

The soup is now ready to serve, and makes at least 6 large servings.

Violet gave Pearl a big Ironstone China tureen that is at least four generations old. It is a delight to use on special occasions, such as when potato soup is served.

I slice 2 or 3 varieties of cheeses, have a bowl of soda or soup crackers, and have either a lettuce salad or a relish plate on the table. I also serve some type of canned or fresh fruit for dessert. Place salad plates and dessert dishes on the table so each person may serve himself.

If you try this soup, be sure to make the egg dumplings. My family feels that the soup is not complete without them and their complaints are long and loud.

In homestead days, we used a small amount of water when cooking the potatoes, and then added a quart of whole milk, brought to a boil, then added the dumplings. This makes an excellent soup, but sometimes the milk might curdle slightly if simmered for 10 minutes. I find that the evaporated milk is just as good and the soup is certainly easier to make.

— My family complains if I do not have enough dumplings, so I make a double batch.

— If you like variety in flavor, dice a stalk of celery into the soup, while cooking the potatoes.

FRIED POTATOES
(Boiled)

Cold boiled potatoes, either diced or sliced were often used for frying. Slice or dice potatoes and plan for one cup per serving. Start with **4 tablespoons of bacon grease** for a **quart of potatoes**, and add more to the pan if necessary, as the potatoes fry. *Do not* put the *grease* on the potatoes, but underneath if more is necessary. Brown, then turn, stir slightly and continue browning, turning and then stirring. They are good!

If you have a weight problem, don't eat too much, and use a vegetable oil instead of bacon grease or lard.

POTATO SALAD #1

We always liked potato salad and it was a must for picnics, school parties, and even for dinner and supper at times. Here is a basic *Vinegar Dressing* for potato salad or green salads.

A really good salad has home made dressing. Put **4 tablespoons vinegar** in a small pan and add enough **water to make one-half cup** liquid. To this add **4 tablespoons butter, 4 tablespoons sugar** and bring to boil, meanwhile stirring.

Have ready **one quart diced boiled potatoes, one small onion diced, three or four hard boiled eggs diced, ½ teaspoon salt, and ¼ teaspoon pepper,** and ¼ teaspoon celery seed. (Celery seed optional). Pour the hot dressing over this mixture and stir. This is a simple but tasty potato salad and is easy to make.

POTATO SALAD #2

Now to make a special dressing for a special salad. Add **two slightly beaten eggs** to the dressing recipe already given and stir constantly while cooking until the dressing has thickened. Use the basic potato salad recipe, but add other ingredients. You might use **diced sweet pickle,** or **sliced green olives,** or **bits of pimento.** There is a wide range of possibilities to enhance the flavor of the potato salad. Be sure the dressing is hot when poured over the potatoes, as the flavor is absorbed more quickly.

The salad may be dressed up for a party by decorating with **strips of pimento,** or **sliced hard boiled eggs,** or **sliced olives,** a **sprig** or two of **parsley,** or a **dash of paprika.**

MASHED POTATO SALAD

One time I was visiting at Uncle Bert and Aunt Hattie's when they were living in Canada. My cousin Lelia and I were helping with dinner and also preparing lunch for the long 70 mile drive by horses and buckboard from Tribune, Saskatchewan, Canada to Medicine Lake,

Montana the next day, for I was going home. I was mashing potatoes when Lelia screamed at me, "Louise, that is the potato salad!" I had done a very good job mashing the salad while Lelia was whipping the mashed potatoes. Aunt Hattie just laughed and said that we would eat it anyway. We ate the mashed potato salad and we liked it.

Sometimes today, I serve a hot, mashed potato salad, with roasted or fried chicken for a buffet dinner and the family enjoys the change.

POTATO SALAD AND BACON

Another salad that I like is made by the first method given, with a slight variation. Prepare the **quart of potatoes** in the usual manner, then **fry several slices of bacon a crispy brown.** Remove all the grease but four tablespoons. Crumble the bacon and set aside. Put **three or four tablespoons vinegar** in a measuring cup, **add enough water to make ½ cup liquid,** pour in the skillet, **add 4 tablespoons sugar,** and bring to boil, add the **potatoes** and **onions** and heat through, add the **crumbled bacon,** mix, and turn into a serving dish. **Eggs** are optional in this dressing recipe.

BAKED POTATOES

We had baked potatoes in the winter time quite often, for the kitchen stove always had a fire in order to help heat the house. The medium size potatoes were well washed and spots trimmed out. It took 1 hour to 1 hour and one-half to bake depending on the temperature of the oven. Each person seasoned his own potato with butter, salt and pepper and sometimes powdered parsley. Grandpa, especially, liked the powdered parsley and used it on many of his foods including baked potatoes.

Any baked potatoes left over were saved for fried or scalloped potatoes.

SCALLOPED POTATOES #1

Mamma sometimes scalloped potatoes by using the raw potatoes and sometimes by using the pre-cooked.

Wash, peel and slice very thin **4 or 5 medium size potatoes.** Grease a 5" x 9" x 3" baking dish. Place **½ inch layer of potatoes in the dish, sprinkle with flour, dot with butter, and salt and pepper lightly.** Continue in this manner until the dish is filled within ½ inch of top. Pour in enough milk to reach the top layer of potatoes, seeing that the flour is soaked. If the dish is too full, the milk will boil over. Place in a 350° oven and cook for a good hour and a half, or longer if the potatoes are not tender.

SCALLOPED POTATOES #2

These potatoes are very good, but I prefer to use **sliced potatoes** that have been boiled. Place the potatoes in the baking dish or casserole in the same fashion as the raw ones — layers of potatoes, seasoned with **salt** and **pepper,** sprinkled with **flour,** dotted with **butter,** and lastly add sufficient **milk** to just barely cover the top layer of potatoes. This second method is just as tasty as the first and will be ready to serve in much less time.

This amount of potatoes will take **2 or 3 tablespoons of butter** (more if you like rich food) and **2 or 3 tablespoons of flour.** I usually put a **cup of whole milk** over the potatoes and then add enough **evaporated milk** to barely cover the top layer. Just the whole milk in a sufficient quantity is all right. The amount of flour varies, for some people prefer the thickened milk to be a thin sauce and others prefer a thicker sauce when the potatoes are served.

For variety, dice onions between the layers of potatoes. At other times, grated cheese spread over the top of the potatoes during the last ten minutes of cooking makes an interesting change. Scalloped potatoes may be both your meat and vegetable dish if you add either generous amounts of diced ham or dried beef to each layer of potatoes.

CREAMED POTATOES

Creamed potatoes may either be made with pre-boiled potatoes or raw potatoes, although I believe the raw potatoes give a better flavor and have more of the nutritional elements since the water in which the potatoes are boiled is retained.

If I use the pre-cooked potatoes, I slice enough **potatoes to fill a quart measure.** Use a two quart kettle for the potatoes, **add ½ cup of hot water,** slowly heat the potatoes to the boiling point, turning carefully as they heat. **Add 1½ cups of milk** and continue heating. In the meanwhile, put **half a cup of milk and 3 tablespoons of either cornstarch or flour** in a pint jar and shake vigorously. This will mix the milk and thickening so there will be no lumps. Put **½ teaspoon of salt** on the potatoes, **a sprinkle of pepper, and 2 tablespoons of butter.** Slowly stir the thickener into the potatoes until the milk thickens.

You could, if you prefer, use a white sauce (instead of the thickener) and slowly pour over the sliced potatoes, stirring as you pour. Either use a double boiler or set the potato kettle in a pan of hot water so they will remain hot until served.

A GOOD BASIC WHITE SAUCE

Heat **1 tablespoon of butter** either in a small kettle or a small skillet and stir in **1 tablespoon of flour.** Stir until well blended then slowly add **1 cup of warm milk** beating constantly until the milk becomes smooth. This may be seasoned with salt and pepper if desired. This makes a thin white sauce.

A medium sauce is made with **2 tablespoons butter, 2 tablespoons flour,** and **1 cup milk.** Use **4 tablespoons butter** and **4 tablespoons flour** for a thick sauce. Follow the same cooking directions as for the thin sauce.

CREAMED POTATOES FROM RAW POTATOES

Slice **a quart of raw potatoes** by using a sharp paring knife or the knife side of your grater. Place the sliced potatoes in a two quart kettle, add **2 or 3 tablespoons butter, 2 cups water,** bring to boil, then lower the heat and simmer with kettle covered until potatoes are tender. **Add a cup or cup and one-half of either whole milk, evaporated milk, or even some cream** if you like rich food. **Make a thickener** by mixing **4 tablespoons flour and ½ cup of water** in a covered pint jar and shake vigorously. When the potatoes come back to the boiling point, add the flour and water as you slowly stir the potatoes. When the potatoes are thickened, pour into a large serving dish, and sprinkle with salt and black pepper. Flaked parsley also makes a good seasoning and makes the food look more attractive.

Some people like their creamed potatoes with a thick gravy and some like it thin so each cook's judgement will vary accordingly and the amount of thickener used will vary.

Creamed potatoes served with hot biscuits and jelly, fried bacon strips or ham, celery, carrot sticks and green onions, plus either fresh or canned fruits and beverage makes a hearty meal.

FRIED POTATOES (RAW)

Sometimes for dinner or supper, Mamma would fry the raw potatoes. We liked the raw potatoes diced, then fried until tender and brown. One method is to heat a ten inch heavy skillet until hot, turn heat back to medium or medium high and put in **2 or 3 tablespoons of lard or bacon grease.** Add **2 cups diced potatoes** and turn when well browned on the underside. Continue cooking at medium heat until browned on the lower side. The layer of potatoes is thin, so should be tender when both sides are well browned. You may either **season with salt and pepper** now or add the seasoning as the potatoes fried. This will serve two people. Cooked in this manner they could be called, "Hashed browns."

Another way to cook these diced potatoes is to gently stir and turn as soon as the potatoes become slightly brown. Continue stirring and turning until they are tender and quite brown. This may require some more grease, but add only a little at a time and put it on the skillet not on the potatoes. These potatoes may be seasoned to taste while either in the process of cooking or when served.

Today, I do not bother to dice the potatoes, but use the big holes on a grater. This is just as good, and certainly is a time saver. The more people you serve, the more potatoes you need. You will also need a bigger skillet for the best results.

Another way to prepare raw fried potatoes is to slice them very thin, using a knife or the slicing side of your grater. Plan on one cup of sliced potatoes for each person served and use either of the two processes already discussed.

MASHED POTATOES

Mashed Potatoes sounds like a very ordinary and common-place dish, but good mashed potatoes are not that simple.

It takes **5 to 6 medium sized potatoes** to make 2 pounds of the peeled potatoes which will be 8 to 10 average servings, so figure the number of people you plan to serve. If they are hearty eaters, such as growing boys, or hard workers, they will want large servings, especially if you serve family style.

Peel and half or quarter the potatoes so they will cook more quickly, **use 2 cups of water** and tightly cover the kettle so the potatoes not covered by water will cook in the steam. Bring to a hard boil, lower to medium heat where they will continue to boil, until the potatoes are very tender when checked with a sharp fork. This will take from 20 to 30 minutes depending on the size of the potato pieces, and the altitude.

You may also use your pressure cooker according to directions. In kettle cooking, you will probably still have 1/2 to 3/4 cups of water left. Part of the water may remain on the potatoes. I either mash the potatoes with an old time potato masher or potato ricer. **Add 2 to 4 tablespoons butter, 1 teaspoon salt,** and have **heated 1 cup of whole milk or more.** I use my electric mixer and beat the potatoes, adding 1/4 cup of milk at a time. Don't add the milk all at once for it may make the mashed potatoes too thin. The final mixture should have a thick, creamy consistency that will stand firmly in soft peaks. If you do not use enough milk, the texture will be dry and grainy. Too much milk will make the potatoes runny.

Some people use cream instead of milk and no butter. This is delicious, but think of the calories!

The sight of just plain mashed potatoes stacked in a bowl is appetizing, but to make a company dish, put 2 or 3 slices of butter on the top, swirl the potatoes around the inside edges of the bowl with a spoon, and sprinkle with paprika.

When we mashed potatoes on the homestead we had a wooden potato masher, how old I do not know. Cracks had formed in the wood and it was very difficult to dig out the potatoes from these cracks when washing. I hated the potato masher when I had to wash dishes.

To beat the potatoes, we used a big slotted spoon, and if we had company, a big kettle of potatoes was really hard work, for we always beat them until they were creamy.

Mamma always made more mashed potatoes than would be eaten and saved what was left over for potato cakes.

POTATO CAKES

Potato cakes are a favorite with my family. Use **2 cups left-over mashed potatoes** or whatever you have, **2 eggs slightly beaten, 2 tablespoons flour, ¼ teaspoon salt, ½ teaspoon of baking powder** and mix well. It may be necessary to add more flour as the potato cakes should be thicker than the batter for pancakes. Their consistency must be such that they will spread out very little when dropped into the hot grease. Shortening may have to be added as the cakes cook, but avoid too much or the food will be greasy.

Heat **3 tablespoons grease** in a large medium or medium hot skillet. Using a tablespoon, drop the potato mixture into the skillet. Dip the back of the spoon in the grease and lightly pat down top of cake. They brown quickly, so be ready to turn with a pancake turner. They may be served as a regular vegetable without further seasoning, and I prefer them this way. Some of the family use syrup or jelly on them.

Another way to make potato cakes is to add more flour to the mixture and make patties to dip in flour and fry. These are very good, but I prefer the first method for taste, and it is easier and quicker to do.

WARMED-UP MASHED POTATOES

Sometimes I warm the mashed potatoes for another meal. I heat them in a double boiler, add a small amount of butter, and just enough hot milk to make a cream mixture that stands in peaks when well beaten. We refrigerate mashed potatoes and keep only a day or two as they spoil easily and could cause food poisoning.

POTATOES BOILED IN JACKETS

One of my kitchen duties was to peel potatoes, and I had to peel enough to cook a big kettle full. We would have boiled potatoes for dinner, or sometimes mashed. There would be fried potatoes or creamed potatoes or potato salad for supper. If enough were left, there would be fried potatoes for breakfast.

Mamma didn't want me to cut myself, so the knife I used didn't have a point and wasn't very sharp. I couldn't peel those potatoes thin enough. Mamma would say, "Louise, if you don't make the peelings thinner, you may go to the poor farm someday." I didn't exactly know what a poor farm was, but I didn't like the idea. I was always glad when Mamma said to boil the potatoes with the jackets on. This was easy. I washed the potatoes, trimmed away any bad spots, put them into a kettle, covered them with hot water, and a tight lid and they boiled until tender when tested with a fork with sharp tines.

Potatoes in their jackets are really good eating. The skins may be removed easily and the potato cut up or mashed on the plate. Season with butter, salt and pepper. These potatoes are also good with a generous serving of milk gravy. If a person does not want to skin the potato, eat both the potato and the skin. The part of the potato next to the skins and the skins have the most nutrients, so I am told. It will be a new but palatable taste sensation.

Milk gravy is delicious on boiled potatoes, mashed potatoes, buttermilk biscuits, and also light bread. Some people even use milk gravy on pancakes.

MILK GRAVY

Melt **4 tablespoons bacon grease** in a large medium hot skillet. Add **6 tablespoons flour,** stir in the hot grease and keep stirring until browned but not burned. Remove from heat. Slowly stir in **1 cup hot water.** When well mixed **add two cups milk,** stirring constantly and return to heat. Cook and stir until well thickened. Season with 1/2 **teaspoon salt** and 1/8 **teaspoon black pepper.** This makes a thick gravy.

A cup and a half of water and the same amount of evaporated milk may be used. An instant milk made according to directions makes acceptable gravy.

I have seen some people take two or three biscuits at one time, break open, place them on the plate, and then cover the biscuits liberally with milk gravy. It takes a big bowl of gravy to take care of a situation like that, so you might want to double the recipe.

NEW PEAS AND POTATO

It was an exciting day when the peas were big enough to eat. Then Grandpa would "grub" around the potato hills to see if there were any new potatoes. "Grubbing" is done by lifting the potato plant and checking under the plant to see if there are any big cracks in the soil. If there are, dig around carefully with your fingers and you will probably find one to three inch potatoes growing not far from the surface. The plant is not disturbed when you take these potatoes.

Now you are set for new peas and potatoes for dinner. Olive and I generally shelled the peas with orders not to eat any, but the temptation was sometimes too much and we would pop some of those sweet, crunchy peas into our mouths. Mamma always seemed to know, though, what we were doing, even if she wasn't looking.

Mamma would scrape the thin skins from the little potatoes, and have them washed and ready for the kettle by the time we had finished the peas.

Mamma placed just enough **water** in the kettle, **a cup or two** to keep the peas and potatoes from boiling dry. She also added **2 or 3 tablespoons of butter.** (Butter added to boiling vegetables will keep the liquid from bubbling over the top of the kettle.) When the peas and potatoes were tender, Mamma added milk and thickener, salt and pepper, simmered for a few minutes longer, then poured them into a large serving bowl.

The first peas and potatoes of the season — they were mouth watering and delicious! We usually had radishes and new onions at the same time.

"We lived near Fort Peck Indian Reservation"

"THREE PEAS AND THREE POTATOES"

One Fourth of July, we celebrated by having dinner at Aunt Ella's and the Doctor's. The grown-ups ate dinner in the shade of the house and the children ate in the shade of a tent made of blankets thrown over the clothes line.

This was really early for much garden stuff, but Aunt Ella had cooked new peas and potatoes. There were plenty for everybody to have a serving of each, but we couldn't fill our plates and have seconds. Aunt Ella, in fun, had said we could have three peas and three potatoes and Harry Fail, the youngest of the group, very seriously took her at her word and carefully counted out three peas and three potatoes.

It was a treat though, to have vegetables that early from the garden. We, of course, had other good things, and all the lemonade we could drink.

New potatoes can be served several ways and all are good— especially if they come early in the vegetable season.

FRIED NEW POTATOES

Boil in **4 cups water,** little **new potatoes** in their jackets. Fry half of them crispy brown with their jackets on in **2 or 3 tablespoons grease,** turning them carefully to brown. Place on a folded paper towel on a hot plate, sprinkle with **salt** and **pepper** and perhaps **flaked parsley** — serve jackets and all. They are very edible and an epicure would enjoy the taste of these new fried potatoes.

CREAMED NEW POTATOES

Skin the remainder of the **boiled new potatoes** and the next day, make a **white sauce,** add the potatoes and heat for dinner. Season with **butter, salt** and **pepper.**

These small potatoes may also be scraped before boiling.

— New potatoes may be soaked in cold water for an hour, then rubbed with a rough towel to remove the skins.

— New potatoes may also be boiled with their jackets on and when cooled the skins may easily be removed.

— Wear rubber gloves when you scrape the raw, new potatoes or your hands will be stained an ugly brown.

— Canned new potatoes are sometimes found on your grocer's shelves. They are good and may be treated as you would new potatoes. But let's face it — they are not quite as good as potatoes right from the garden.

One method for creaming new potatoes is to place a **cup of water** and a generous **quart of already cooked potatoes** in a 2 quart kettle. Add **2 or 3 tablespoons butter,** according to taste, ½ **teaspoon of salt** and ¼ **teaspoon of pepper.** Bring to boil, and heat all potatoes thoroughly by turning in the hot liquid. To this add **a cup of evaporated milk** and **thickener,** how much depends on whether you want a thin or thick sauce for your potatoes. Add the thickener slowly stirring constantly so the gravy or sauce will not be lumpy.

BASKET SOCIAL

I looked forward with both great excitement and a certain amount of dread to a basket social. These socials were used as a method of community money making as well as a social event.

We practiced and practiced our recitations or speeches, our plays, and marching drills and songs in preparation for the program. The school children took the great news home. That was the advertising, and soon the neighbors for miles around knew about the program and the basket social. At school all the girls planned to take a box. A basket for the little girls was usually a shoe box, covered with colored crepe paper and perhaps a few pasted on decorations.

The big girls and the ladies in the community made really beautiful boxes, some square, some oblong, some round, some tall. They were covered with crepe paper, and crepe paper flowers. Some looked like big flower baskets and other ornate houses and castles. In reality the boxes and baskets showed a great deal of imagination and ingenuity, and many hours of hard work.

The box or basket, which was filled with a hearty lunch or supper, was auctioned off to a man that bid the highest and he then ate supper with the owner of the box.

Mamma always had plenty of good food for two people in our boxes, fried chicken, ground meat sandwiches, pickles, deviled eggs, potato salad, celery, cake or pie and either apples, oranges, or bananas.

As people arrived, the baskets were placed on a table in front of the room so they could be seen by everybody. There was a great deal of looking and speculating about the ownership of the box, especially if any of the older girls had a fellow or was "going steady." Some of the men even picked up a box to see if it was heavy enough to have a big lunch.

My cousin Helen, one of the older girls, was quite popular. When she started going with Alfred, all the fellows in the neighborhood were ready to make him bid high for her basket.

The school house was lighted by half a dozen reflector kerosene wall lamps and some lanterns brought in by community members. First came the school program, followed by dancing, then the auctioning of the baskets and supper, then more dancing, sometimes until daylight. The seats were pushed back around the wall. There was the smell of coffee boiling in a big wash boiler on a kerosene stove in front of the room. The fiddler put away his instrument, and the auctioneer started selling baskets. The bidding generally didn't go very high for the family

men. Some of the bachelors that weren't going with a special girl would buy the boxes of the little girls — sometimes two or three.

At this one particular box supper, the fellows found out which was Helen's box and when the bidding started, they kept forcing the bid higher and higher. Helen with her heavy dark braids wound around her head, her cheeks rosy, sat primly in her long gathered gray handmade dress with the long sleeves and high neck line and waited and listened, as did all of us. The auctioneer would joke with the men and badger them into making higher and higher bids.

The bid was forced up and up and up until Alfred had to pay $8.00. That was a vast amount of money in those days for a young fellow to spend on his girl.

After the boxes were sold, people sat around in couples and groups and had supper. Sometimes, two or three families would eat together, having brought extra food for the smaller children. I was frightened, but sat there very quietly watching my manners, still enjoying the food, talking very little. Olive refused point blank to eat with the bachelor that bought her box and stayed right with Mamma.

After supper, we generally went home, but many stayed to dance, far into the early morning. I always hated to leave the dances. When I was small, I was entranced, sitting and watching the dancers and listening to the music. They did the one step, the two step, the three step, the schottische, Virginia reel, the polka and the old time waltz, and square dances. Mamma taught Olive and me to waltz, and it was fun to whirl and swirl to the gay music. Mamma would entertain us with a very lively jig at home, but she was always very sedate and proper in public.

I remember when the three step became popular. We practiced and practiced it at school.

I wanted so badly to learn all the dances, and it wasn't too long until I knew most of them. Those old fiddlers would almost make their fiddles talk. (They were fiddles, not violins.) They could play all night without tiring, their fiddle bows flying, toes tapping, bodies swaying, long mustaches flip-flopping to the beat of the music.

When Mamma had a box supper or basket social at her school, she would use the money to buy library books. She was responsible for starting several libraries, as she taught all through that section of the country. Sometimes schools would only last 3 months, and then she would go on to another one that was just starting.

I could hardly wait for the books to come — the Old Greek and Roman myths, the Alger books, Winston Churchill's Richard Carvel and other historical novels; Marion and His Men; The Swamp Fox; The Green Mountain Boys; The Little Colonel Books; Steward Edward White's animal stories. I read the Elsie books, read and reread them and loved them all. Of course, I didn't know some of the words, but I got a great deal by context and Mamma was very patient when I asked about words. We had phonics at school and that helped.

FRIED CHICKEN

Fried chicken was an important part of many of our meals as well as basket socials. I never tired of it. We had a large, iron skillet that we used when we fried chicken.

Mamma was very busy with the program at school one day when we were having a basket social. After school, a neighbor took me home and

I got the lunches ready for Mamma's, Olive's, and my baskets. These were already decorated, so I just had to prepare the food. A chocolate cake had been baked, but I had to catch, dress, cut up and fry the chicken and make deviled eggs.

I had to work hard to cut up the chicken, as I was 12 at the time and small for my age.

I put Mamma's heavy iron skillet on the stove and spooned in enough lard to make **three inches of melted grease.** When the grease was medium hot, I put in the **pieces of chicken which had been lightly salted,** (about one teaspoon for a whole chicken) then **rolled in flour.** I poked many holes in the liver with a sharp fork to keep it from splattering and popping the hot grease onto my hand. The chicken cooked 15 to 20 minutes or until it was well browned, then I turned it and cooked the other side for approximately the same time. The skillet was covered, but the lid does not fit tightly. Some tight lids will make the chicken steam. I prefer the chicken to be crisp.

By 6:30 p.m., the neighbor arrived to take me back to the school house. The baskets were packed with the food carefully wrapped in waxed paper. I had added two of Mamma's pretty napkins to each box and had three glasses for water and three cups for coffee. I had brushed and plaited my hair, but left my hair bows for Mamma to tie on. My gray challis dress had a fitted bodice, long sleeves and a full skirt halfway to my ankles. I had cuffbands on the sleeves and a yoke and high neck band of dark red velvet. Long black stockings and high button shoes completed my outfit.

The horses pulled the buggy briskly along the dusty road. I practiced my poem over and over to myself, so I would not forget, when my turn on the program came.

TO CUT UP A CHICKEN

Today, I buy the whole fryer at the market as it is cheaper. I use the following process to prepare the chicken for the frying pan.

First pull the leg away from the body and with a strong sharp butcher knife, cut through the skin and meat between the body and the leg down to the joint. Press the leg down away from the body and work the knife between the bone joints, then cut through the remaining flesh. Take off both legs then separate the thigh from the lower leg. Do this by pulling the thigh and leg pieces backward from the joint. This snaps the joint open. Cut down to the joint and insert the knife point between the bones and then cut on through.

The wings are pulled back from the body, the joints broken open and the wings cut off. The wing has three sections, the tip is tucked under the end of the big section forming a triangle. This keeps the wing in place for frying.

Next cut off the pulley bone. Feel along the breast bone with your finger until you reach the highest point. Cut down from this point as close to the body bones as possible toward the neck, then break and cut away the "pulley bone." This is white meat. Next separate the back from the upper part of the body. Pull up the breast part and cut completely through to and through the back bone.

The breast and rib parts may now be cut into two or three pieces. I usually cut into three pieces.

Cut off the ribs close to the breast bone on both sides. Then divide the ribs at the back bone. This gives two rib pieces with quite a little white meat. The breast as it is, makes a very generous piece of white meat, or it may be halved by splitting down the middle — bone and meat. The back is left. Just flatten this out by pushing down on the center of the back and breaking the bones next to the back bone. The meat cooks better.

If the butcher has left the little oil sack on at the base of the tail remove it, as it will make the chicken oily when cooked. It may make the chicken taste strong.

I SEW A DRESS

At the beginning of World War I, Mamma decided I should take sewing lessons. I was doing my own ironing (except my best dresses), darning my stockings, sewing on buttons, and now it was time for me to make a dress.

Cousin Lillie was a dress-maker and did beautiful needlework, so she was my teacher. She was very patient. She had to be, as I was very inept, but I finally made a brown gingham dress, trimmed with brown and blue plaid. I was very proud of that dress, and wore it on every occasion. Although I didn't enjoy the sewing I did enjoy staying with Cousin Lillie for a few days, and I especially enjoyed her Liberty pancakes.

At the time, we were strictly rationed as to flour, and sugar and used various substitutes. Cousin Lillie had found this Liberty pancake recipe in a magazine.

LIBERTY PANCAKES

The original recipe was to soak **3 cups of rolled oats overnight in sour milk** — enough milk to cover the oats. (Rolled oats or oatmeal at that time was not pre-cooked and took hours to cook for the table as a cereal.) The next morning, **add 1 cup corn meal, 1 cup flour, 1 teaspoon salt, 2 teaspoons baking powder, 2 eggs, ¼ cup bacon drippings, enough more milk to make a nice batter,** and **1 heaping teaspoon soda** or more if milk is quite sour.

The following adjustment makes this pancake recipe more adaptable for present day use. If you use long cooking oatmeal by all means soak all night in buttermilk, but it is not necessary to soak the one-minute variety.

The original recipe serves several people, so I have adjusted it to serve four.

1 cup oatmeal (minute)
2½ cups buttermilk or perhaps a little more depending on the absorption into the oatmeal
½ cup flour
½ cup cornmeal
1 tablespoon bacon drippings, oil, or melted butter
1 teaspoon baking powder
½ teaspoon soda
1 egg

Beat the egg before adding to the batter, then beat the batter hard or use electric mixer for 2 minutes. The batter should have the consistency of thick catsup.

Cook on an iron griddle or skillet at medium heat. When the cake begins to bubble and the edges turn brown the cakes are ready to turn. These pancakes take longer to cook than regular flour cakes, so remember to have medium heat, otherwise they will get too brown and not be quite done inside. An iron skillet or iron griddle requires very little shortening or oil.

Use honey, jelly, or white Karo on the pancakes. The white Karo seems just right to me. Have a choice of fresh fruits in an attractive bowl, and serve either bacon, ham or scrambled eggs with the cakes.

WHERE THE WILD PLUMS GROW

Wild plums were difficult to get. We had to go farther west or south, but we were delighted when we had an opportunity to get some, or maybe we were given a couple of gallons by some neighbor.

Wild plums sometimes ripen to a deep red, a bright red, an orange and some are even yellow. Some are quite tart and others are very sweet and edible. They are usually oval, but some are round and they are approximately the size of the average green seedless grapes.

Uncle Sid and family, when a new homestead law came in, moved down into the Sarpy country out of Hardin near the Crow Indian Reservation. We would visit there in the fall and take home enough wild plums for pies and winter canning.

The wild plum is hard to seed. The following makes this job easier. Wash and boil a large kettle full of plums with enough water to just come to the top of the fruit. The plums will become tender and will split. Take off the stove and let stand until cool.

WILD PLUM PIE

The seeds slip out easily with a little pressure of the fingers and soon there are enough seeded plums for the pie. Take **3 cups full of plums plus ¼ cup juice, 1 to 1½ cups sugar, 3 tablespoons flour, 1 egg, slightly beaten, and ½ teaspoon salt.** Mix thoroughly and pour into an **unbaked 9" pie crust, cover with the top crust.** Bake in a pre-heated oven at 425° for 10 minutes, then turn down heat and finish baking at 375° for 35 minutes.

An excellent pie for Sunday dinner or for that matter any dinner! What is more, you picked those plums yourself!

It's fun to get your food from the land. Take a substantial lunch and plenty of water, or coffee and go to the brakes or low hills where the plum trees grow. The warm earth, the bright blue sky, the scurrying white clouds, golden rod swaying on tall stalks, and an occasional wild aster with its deep lavendar petals are unforgettable pictures. Hunting for another and another tree, for just another bucket of plums — tasting and eating that rich, tangy plum is fascinating.

Wild plum jam is good at any time and especially good with hot bread.

WILD PLUM JAM

After putting **two quarts of cooked wild plums** through the colander, measure the pulp and juice into a large kettle and add the **same amount of sugar.** Bring to a boil and boil slowly, stirring very often. The mixture is thick and scorches easily. When it drops from the spoon in double drops or thickens quickly when dropped onto a chilled saucer, pour into hot sterilized pint jars or jelly glasses. The fruit jars may be sealed and the jelly glasses covered with parowax.

WILD PLUM PRESERVES

Wild plum preserves are almost as good as the cherry preserves that Elsie brought from Indiana.

Begin with **3 cups of the cooked pitted plums** and **1 cup juice.** Add **4 cups of sugar.** Slowly simmer until the juice becomes thick as honey. Can in sterilized hot half pint or pint jars. These may be opened for special occasions, or keep a few on hand for a Christmas present for a shut-in friend.

WILD PLUM JELLY

Jelly is made by mixing the **strained juice** with an **equal amount of sugar** and boiling until the double drops fall from a spoon. This is a beautiful, light red jelly that has a sharp, sweet taste.

WILD PLUM SYRUP

Wild plum syrup served hot is good on pancakes and is a savory addition to puddings and custards. The beautiful red syrup is delicious dribbled over a dish of vanilla ice cream.

Boil **equal amounts** of **strained juice** and **sugar** until it begins to thicken, and you then have this colorful syrup which may be canned for later use.

WILD PLUM COBBLER

A fruit cobbler is always good and the wild plum is especially delicious made into a cobbler. Use **4 cups of sweetened fruit** in a 8" x 8" x 3" baking dish. Cover with **rolled dough (biscuit)** cut in squares or in biscuit rounds and bake in a 450° oven for 20 minutes, serve hot with rich milk or cream. It's very appetizing!

PLUM SAUCE AND DROP DUMPLINGS

Take **4 cups of seeded wild plums** and **4 cups of juice,** make very sweet and bring to a boil in a large kettle. "Very Sweet" depends, of course, upon the individual, but I use **2 to 3 cups (or even 4) of sugar,** depending upon the natural sugar in the plums. Drop the dumpling dough by teaspoonful into the hot fruit. Cover the kettle tightly and simmer for 15 minutes.

Serve this hot dessert with rich milk, cream or a hard sauce. It is very savory. Don't eat too big a dinner, so you may have two servings! Comment: — I have given the methods of making jams, jellies, and preserves that Mamma used as my sister and I grew up. The taste I think is superior to the present method of processing our jams and jellies with pectin, but the pectin is very good and certainly much easier and quicker to do.

I have spoken of double drops falling from side of the spoon when making jams and jellies. Those double drops join and form a sheet when the jelly or jam is done.

CHOW-CHOW
(It's a pickle, not a dog)

I prepare my vegetables for chow-chow early the evening before the actual canning process. I wash **8 pounds of very green tomatoes** and trim off rusty and rough spots, cut into approximately 2 inch chunks, and grind with a food chopper. **Salt** the ground tomatoes until they have a strong salt taste. When grinding the tomatoes have a "catch-pan" ready under the grinder as the tomatoes are very juicy.

Wash, trim, cut into chunks and grind **5 green peppers, 3 red peppers,** and **2 pounds of onions.** Mix at least **¼ cup of salt** into this mixture, and make sure that it has a strong salt flavor. More salt may have to be added.

Grate **4 pounds of cabbage** and add salt. Allow these vegetables to stand for an hour and squeeze out all the liquid. Before bedtime, squeeze again getting all moisture possible out.

I put these ground vegetables all together in a large crockery jar or stainless steel roaster.

The following morning, I clean and dice very fine **one large bunch of celery.** More juice was formed in the ground and grated vegetables and this time be very sure to remove it by squeezing very hard. The men's hands seem to be stronger, so have the man of the house take his turn. Sometimes I place the ground mixture in a cloth bag and by twisting the top very tight and pressing hard, I am able to get out more juice. If all these juices are not squeezed out, the chow-chow may be bitter.

Place the vegetables in a large kettle, preferably stainless steel, or if you do not have a big one, 2 smaller ones will do.

Add **4 ounces of white mustard seed, 2 ounces of celery seed, 4 cups water, 4 cups apple cider vinegar** and **4 cups of sugar.** Mix well, and bring to a boil over medium heat. Simmer and stir for 30 minutes. There should be sufficient liquid to make these pickles very moist, but not runny.

Taste the relish as it cooks and if there seems to be enough vinegar, add only water to keep the pickles moist. If you like a vinegary pickle, add just a little more vinegar with the water. Check for the sugar, too. I like a sweet pickle, so I add one or two more cups of sugar. So much of this depends on the individual, but my family all like the vinegary sweet taste of these mixed pickles.

Can in sterilized pint or half-pint self-sealing jars. When canning pickles or any food, be sure to check top of jar for nicks in the glass. The top of the jar must be absolutely smooth, so there may be no air seepage that could cause food spoilage. It is cheaper to throw away the jar than to have spoiled food.

When canning, you sometimes find that you have taken most of the juice before getting to the bottom of the kettle and the pickles are too dry. If so, add some water, bring to a good boil to sterilize, then complete the canning.

The sharp aroma of the cooking mixed pickles, spices, sugar and vinegar drift through the house and out the open windows. Company will come just to see what you are doing, and want to taste, then ask for the recipe.

Chow-chow is excellent as a relish for fish and meat dishes. When mixed with ground meat it makes a hearty sandwich. Other suggestions for use would be in egg salad, deviled eggs, potato salad, and meat loaf.

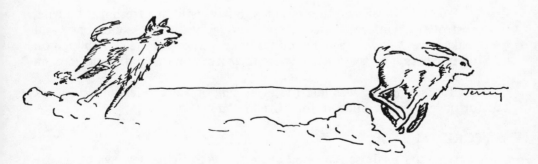

BUTCHERING TIME

Hog butchering came late in the fall when the weather was cold enough that the meat would not spoil before it was processed.

Butchering day was very exciting. People were all over the place for relatives or neighbors and their families came to help. Olive and I got as close to the "butchering" as we could for we wanted to see everything. We were well bundled in heavy coats, high buckled overshoes, long underwear, long black stockings, sateen bloomers, bright long stocking caps with the tassel end around our necks and warm mittens.

Aunt Ella was in the house helping Mamma get dinner. James and Violet were helping Olive and I "watch."

After the hog was butchered, we carried the liver and heart into the house, where it was soaked in cold salted water.

FRIED LIVER

Sliced fresh liver is very good dipped in flour, well salted and peppered and fried in plenty of grease. But one word of warning: don't eat too much, because you might have to make several trips to the little house out back. It is very impractical when the weather is cold.

The hog was cut up into sections and hung until the next day to thoroughly chill. Great kettles of fat were taken into the pantry to be cut into inch squares for rendering into lard.

The next day the shoulders and hams were cut off, the ribs cut into short ribs for baking, the back sectioned for baking or roasting. The fresh side meat was stripped from the ribs (same as bacon, but not cured), to be used fresh or to make salt pork and bacon.

In the late afternoon the aunts, uncles, cousins, and neighbors went home with generous amounts of fresh meat. They shared with us when their "butchering" day came.

HOMESTEAD DEEP FREEZE

We had no refrigeration systems, but we still had fresh meat during most of the winter months. After thoroughly cooling, some roasts and steaks were well wrapped and either hung in the coal shed or up high on the north side of the house, where they froze and would remain frozen for several weeks.

Butchering day was just the beginning of a great deal of hard work for the grownups, and fun for Olive and me.

PORK SAUSAGE

Grandpa made sausage and again we were right there watching. He took all the meat scraps from the neck, head, back, sides, and lower legs and ground this meat. The seasoning of the sausage was the fun part. Grandpa put some **sage**, some **salt**, and some **pepper** on the ground meat and mixed it thoroughly. He then made three little patties of sausage and fried them. There was a patty apiece for Olive and me and one for him. If there wasn't enough seasoning, he would add some more and then fry some more patties.

Generally, he was satisfied the second time, but the sausage must be just right, so it might be necessary to sage, pepper and salt again. He liked a mild sausage, so was very careful not to put in too much seasoning. He would eat his patty of sausage very slowly and critically — analyzing every taste. Olive and I would try to do the same. (For special occasions, I buy fresh pork at a butcher shop, grind it and do my own seasoning. It tastes just like the sausage Grandpa used to make.)

A door in the front of the kitchen stove opened into the fire box and hot ashes. Grandpa buried the tail and ears of the pig in these hot ashes and roasted them. They would become semi-burnt and crispy and we almost quarreled over which one would have the tail or the ear.

Grandpa fixed apples to roast for us on a long strong string fastened to the ceiling. The string would be tied to the stem of the apple, and then Grandpa started the apple turning before the hot coals in the fire box. It turned one way for awhile and twisted up the string and then turned back and untwisted it. The apple roasted as it turned. When the apples were finally roasted, we were given a bowl and spoon apiece for our own particular apple. Sometimes there was cream. These apples were juicy and succulent, in other words, absolutely wonderful.

LARD MAKING

Mamma made the lard and that was very interesting, too. She cut up pounds and pounds of fat into 1 to 2 inch chunks and put it in big kettles and slowly cooked the grease out of the fat.

She put a very small amount of water in the bottom at first to prevent the fat from scorching before the grease began forming. The fat had to be kept at low heat and stirred often to keep from burning. Overheating of the lard makes it dark, and sometimes coarse and greasy.

No fat or lard was poured off until all grease was cooked out or rendered out of the fat pieces and no moisture remained. The part of the fat pieces left was called "cracklings."

The grease or liquid fat was strained through two or three thickness of cloth into pails. This liquid fat when cooled was the lard. It was tightly covered and stored in a dark cool place. This was a year's supply of lard.

The cracklings were good to eat, but they were very, very rich. Olive and I had upset stomachs from eating cracklings more than once.

Cracklings put through the meat grinder, are savory substitutes for lard in both buttermilk biscuits and corn bread. It is necessary to use one-fourth more of the cracklings than lard as they are not pure fat.

Another fun thing at butchering time was the bladder balloons that

Grandpa made. He washed the bladder thoroughly, tied up one end, and blew it up and tied the other opening tight. It made a wonderful balloon that was long lasting and practically unbreakable.

If two hogs were butchered, both Olive and I got a balloon, but if only one was butchered, Olive got the balloon because she was smaller than I.

Of course, we ate fresh sausage, but Mamma fried the remainder, packed it in crocks, then covered it with hot grease. When the grease hardened, it kept out the air and made a protective coating that preserved the meat.

Fried sausage sometimes was packed into quart jars, 1 cup of hot grease added, the jar sealed then turned upside down. When the grease hardened the solid fat kept out the air and the sausage remained good for a few months.

PIGS FEET AND HOCKS AND SAUERKRAUT

The pig feet and hocks were scraped and singed. Mamma cooked the pig's feet and hocks in a big kettle until tender, removed the skin, added kraut and cooked some more. That savory smell was like a magnet drawing us into the kitchen. We had baked potatoes, corn bread, sliced onion and stewed fruit for dessert.

CURING HAM AND BACON

Hams and bacon may be cured by either the dry cure or brine method. Grandpa cured his bacon and hams with the dry cure.

If you have a small amount of pork to process, the following proportions are very workable. Large scale meat processing increases the amount of the curing mixture in proportion to the amount of meat to be cured.

Fifty pounds of meat requires **4 pounds of salt, 1 pound sugar** and **1 ounce of saltpeter.** Mix the salt, sugar, and saltpeter thoroughly and set half of the mixture aside for later use.

The pork, after butchering, is allowed to hang overnight at temperatures between 36° and 40° — no part of the animal should be allowed to touch as this prevents proper cooling and may cause spoilage since pork spoils very easily. Let the carcass hang in a cool room (36° to 40°) or in cold storage for 24 hours before cutting. Do not allow it to freeze as the salt will not penetrate frozen meat.

Bacon can be covered and rubbed only once with the salt allotted to it. Thin bacon needs less salt than thick bacon. The salt is rubbed over the entire surface of the meat.

Hams are thicker so be sure they are covered with about 1/8-inch of salt, and salt poked down around the ends of the bone. In 6 or 8 days, add the remainder of the salt. Cure the bacon or keep in salt for 1½ days to the pound and the hams and shoulders for 2 days at least to the pound.

After the meat is dry cured, it may be smoked. In Indiana, Grandpa had a smoke house and he smoked the meat. He then stored the cured hams and bacon in the smoke house.

In Montana, he had no smoke house, so after the meat was cured he rubbed it with liquid smoke to give the smoked taste. He brushed the liquid smoke generously on the hams, and repeated it in 6 to 8 days. The bacon was brushed once lightly as the poundage is much less.

After the hams and bacon are cured and smoked, they were wrapped in heavy paper and slipped into a sugar or flour sack.

Some of the homesteaders made a thick flour and water paste which they spread heavily over the cloth sack. They peppered this liberally with black pepper to discourage flies and insects. Some placed cheese cloth over the bacon and hams and plastered them with heavy flour paste and added either red or black pepper or both, then allowed the paste to dry.

A heavy cord was tied firmly around the meat to hang it from the rafters in a store room.

MAKING SALT PORK

Salt pork is good, and really very easy to make. Take thick slabs of bacon meat, preferrably with considerable fat, allow to cool to 40° or some less, cover with at least ½ inch salt and allow to stand several days. After about 20 days, cut a slice of meat, fry, and taste to see if the salt has penetrated all parts. If it has, store the salt pork in a stone jar or wooden barrel. Place a layer of salt, then a layer of pork, and continue alternating the layers until all the meat has been stored. You can purchase a commercial cure salt.

Salt pork may be cooked in beans and is also good fried.

If you are cooking a big kettle of beans, the salt pork may be used just as it is, as it provides the salt for the beans. If you plan to use several slices of the pork in the beans, you may have to "freshen" it some by placing in cold water, and bringing the water to a boil. Pour off the water.

This will remove much of the extra salt, and the pork may then be used in the beans.

FRYING SALT PORK

To fry salt pork, parboil the slices of pork by placing in cold water and bringing to a boil. Pour off the water and repeat the process two or three times, each time putting on fresh water.

When the pork has been freshened sufficiently, dip or roll it in flour, then put it into a slightly greased skillet and fry to a golden brown. This makes a very good breakfast dish.

Aunt Ella served fried salt pork with fried or scrambled eggs, fried potatoes, hot biscuits, milk gravy, buffalo berry jelly, and a dish of prunes with a choice of milk or coffee.

BOILED HAM

Boiled ham, baked ham, fried ham, and even ham in meat loaf were some of the ways we used that good ham Grandpa made.

A 5 or 6 pound piece of ham was cut from a big ham, placed in a large kettle covered with cold water, brought to a boil and simmered for 10 minutes. We poured off this water since it was used for a freshner, then added fresh water. After bringing it to a boil, the heat was lowered and the meat simmered until tender.

Home cured ham is delicious served for dinner by slicing into generous servings and piled on a meat platter. Both potatoes and cabbage added to the liquid and cooked with the ham make a hearty dinner.

We used the left over ham sliced cold for supper or in sandwiches for the school lunch bucket. A plain ham sandwich is good, but it is just a little better when it is garnished with chow-chow or beet relish.

FRIED HAM

Mamma fried ham for breakfast, dinner, or supper. She sliced the ham, placed it in a large skillet, covered with cold water, brought it to a boil and simmered it for 2 or 3 minutes. Then she drained off water.

I parboil any ham that I fry and home cured ham may have to be freshened a couple of times since it usually has more salt than ham purchased at the meat market.

Pour off the water after freshening, and place 2 or 3 tablespoons of shortening in the skillet. Cook the ham rather slowly, around 250° to 300° until light brown on both sides. If you are really in a hurry, set the heat to 350°.

If it is ham and eggs and hot biscuits for breakfast, fry your eggs in another pan because they may stick to the ham skillet.

HAM GRAVY

Here is a gravy that we enjoy. After placing the ham on a serving platter, allow the skillet to heat a minute or two to brown the grease, then pour in a cup of water. Heat for 3 minutes stirring as the liquid boils. Small particles of ham and the grease mix with the boiling water. This makes a very delicious brown juice to spoon over open halves of biscuits. Be judicious in the amount of the water you use for this gravy, so you will not have too thin a mixture. The more fryings, the more water.

BAKED HAM

The tantalizing odor of baking ham was like a magnet that drew us to the kitchen and we always coaxed for a bite of that crusty brown roast.

Boil the ham until amost tender before you bake it. The water should almost cover the ham. Home cured ham may be salty and have acquired a strong taste from storage. If you feel that it may be strong, allow it to cook for a few minutes in the first water; pour that water off and almost cover ham again and cook. I boil a store purchased ham before baking. The water from a boiled ham is good to use in making bean soup.

Plan to place the ham in a lightly greased baking pan with a cup of water an hour before dinner, and bake slowly for that hour. Make certain sufficient enough moisture remains in the pan to keep the meat from sticking and burning.

The ham may be turned occasionally as it bakes, or it may be basted.

Mamma baked the ham just as it was without any frills. Sometimes I like a change and score the ham in 2 inch squares across the top, place pineapple slices on it and top with generous portions of brown sugar, using the pineapple juice for moisture in the pan. When baked, the entire piece of ham is placed on a meat platter, cut and served at the table. Various other fruit juices are good.

Either cold baked ham or warmed up ham is good for another meal, and it is so good in sandwiches.

MEAT LOAF

Another way to use ham scraps is to add a cup or two of ground ham to a meat loaf.

Our homestead meat loaves could vary anywhere from two to four pounds in size.

The following proportions make a very good two pound meat loaf.

Grind nearly **2 pounds raw meat** through the food chopper. Put the ground meat into a **2 quart mixing bowl**, add **1 cup cracker** or **bread crumps, 1 teaspoon salt, ¼ teaspoon pepper, 2 eggs** and **a cup of milk, or 1 cup of a meat broth** or **bouillon.** Stir well, then pat the mixture into loaf shape in a greased pan, pour a little water into the pan (½ cup) and place in a medium hot oven. Bake until done, approximately an hour. That crusty brown meat loaf is moist and savory. Bake potatoes while the loaf is cooking and serve with cole slaw. Finish the meal with apple pie.

We all liked meat loaf dinners. Sliced meat loaf warmed up in milk gravy with hot buttermilk biscuits and boiled cabbage is an appetizing meal.

I liked thin slices of meat loaf in sandwiches spread with chow-chow for my school lunches. We always had homemade bread.

There are many variations for a good meat loaf. They may be a combination of beef and ham or half fresh beef and half fresh pork.

VARIETIES OF MEAT LOAF

You may use **oatmeal** instead of cracker crumbs. **One-fourth cup diced onion,** or **diced green pepper** adds variety. My daughter, Pearl, uses ½ cup of chow-chow in her meat loaf. Sometimes instead of milk or broth I use **tomato juice** for a liquid. **A can of mushrooms,** or ½ **pound of fresh mushrooms** baked in the ground meat, makes a company main dish.

If you have errands to do and will be away several hours, prepare a meat loaf, wash potatoes for baking, and place in a cold oven. Set your oven timer (allow an hour and 15 minutes) and forget dinner. The first person home puts a vegetable on the stove to cook, sets the table and makes a salad.

BEEF BUTCHERING

Beef butchering was almost, but not quite as much fun as the butchering of the hogs. The animal would be slaughtered, skinned, dressed-out (the entrails removed) and then pulled up to cool out the body heat. It cooled for 24 to 48 hours before it was finally cut for eating and curing.

A generous amount of beef went home with whoever helped Grandpa butcher. Some of the beef was cut into roasts, boils, and steaks for immediate use. It was generally cold enough at butchering time that there was no danger of spoilage. Mamma boiled the neck and bone pieces, for mincemeat, hash, and stews. The meat was stripped from the ribs for boiling. Sometimes, the ribs were sawed into "short ribs" and baked. The back bone was cut into sections for large roasts.

The quarters that were not used immediately were wrapped in old sheets or stored in 100 pound flour sacks and hung high on the north side of the house with the pork. This meat would remain frozen for weeks and would only be taken down to saw off roasts or steaks.

No door was ever locked on the homestead, and nothing was ever stolen, not even our meat.

MAKING DRIED BEEF

Twenty pounds of beef from the round may be prepared for drying by using the following proportions to cure the meat – **2 cups salt, ½ pound brown sugar** and **1 teaspoon saltpeter** or buy the prepared sugar cure.

Divide the mixture into three equal portions. Place the meat in a large bowl. Rub thoroughly on all sides with one portion. Allow to stand for 24 hours. On the second and third days using the second and third portions, rub the meat. Leave the meat in the bowl, but turn several times each day for seven days.

Hang up meat to drip dry, and continue drying for six weeks or longer if necessary.

The meat may now be stored in a cool place.

Malcolm dries venison and elk meat in the same manner. When the meat is cured, he cuts it into very thin slices, packages it, and stores in the deep freeze. Meat dried in this manner is very good.

When the beef had stood long enough in the salt, sugar, and saltpeter, Grandpa would rub liquid smoke on it, and then he would run a heavy string between the hock-bone and tendon and hang the meat behind the stove in the front room to dry. When the beef was dry, he would cut with a very sharp knife thin slices of meat. It was semi-dry and chewy and had the sharp tang of the curing condiments adding a zesty flavor.

This dried beef would keep indefinitely, of course getting some drier, but the good chewy taste remained. Dried beef has other uses than just to eat it as is.

GRAVY AND DRIED BEEF

Dice a **cup full of dried beef** and simmer it in **two cups of water** for nearly an hour. Make a large **skillet of milk gravy** and just before meal time, pour the cooked dried beef into the milk gravy and cook slowly, stirring constantly, for five minutes and serve with buttermilk biscuits hot from the oven.

FRIED STEAK

Both Mamma and Elsie could fry a tender steak. Here's how they did it: lay the meat out on a bread board, sprinkle it heavily with **flour,** add **salt** and **pepper,** then pound the flour into the meat with either the back of a heavy knife or the edge of a heavy saucer. Turn the steak over, flour and pound the other side of the steak thoroughly, and fry in **4 or 5 tablespoons of fat** at medium high heat. Serve when well browned on both sides. Use 3 or 4 tablespoons of the fryings to make gravy. I like breaded tomatoes, mashed potatoes, hot biscuits, and cold cabbage with steak.

One way to prepare fat for frying the steak is to dice either suet or tallow and cook out the fat. Dip out the brown chunks of fat and fry the steaks. If the diced bits of fat are small, well browned and crisp, they may be added to the gravy for a variety in flavor.

BEEF ROAST

Mamma's beef roasts were extra special. Generally, she would roast **6 to 8 pounds of meat** at a time. She would season the meat with **salt** and **pepper** and rub **flour** into the top of the roast. She would put **3 or 4 cups of water** or more into the bread pan and put the roast into a medium hot oven. When the top was browned she would turn the meat over. She floured and seasoned the other side and continued baking or roasting. If the water had evaporated, she added more. She continued turning the meat or basting it until it was done. It took 5 to 6 hours to cook the meat, for after the meat was browned, she kept a slow fire in the kitchen stove.

The flour on the roast kept the meat from becoming hard and dry, helped it brown evenly, thickened the water and juice around the roast, and made a superb gravy.

The large roast was served fresh from the baking pan, warmed up two or three times, then sliced cold for supper, and finally the remains were ground and made into hash. Nothing was ever wasted.

BAKED BEEF SQUARES

Cut some of the tougher pieces of meat, like the **brisket** and lower legs, into **2 and 3 inch squares**, dip in **flour** and brown in **3 or 4 tablespoons of fat** at medium high heat. Leave in frying pan, add **1 to 2 teaspoons salt** and **¼ teaspoon black pepper**, sprinkle with **more flour**, and perhaps add another **tablespoon or two of fat**. Turn, add flour and brown two or three times. **Cover with water** and slightly stir as a thick gravy forms. Next, cover the pan tightly and put in the oven to bake slowly for two or three hours or until the meat is very tender. This method of cooking makes a very savory dish, served with hot cabbage and baked potatoes.

The average beef animal butchered on the farm will have very few cuts of tough beef it if is cut across the grain of the meat.

SANDWICH SPREAD

Sometimes when Mamma had ground cooked meat, she would make a sandwich spread.

Use **3 cups of ground meat** — this could be either pork or beef, **1 cup chow-chow,** and **one basic cooked dressing recipe** with the **two eggs** added for dressing thickener. Use **salt** and **pepper** to taste. **One-fourth cup diced raw onion** or **celery** or both added to this mixture gives variety to the sandwiches. Just use a little practical imagination and ground cooked meat can give you many tasty versions for sandwiches.

Beef fat or suet was not used up in the family cooking, as we did not like the taste of cold tallow. We used what we could and the rest was occasionally given to the dog, the cats, and the chickens for part of their winter feed.

TRIPE

When a beef animal was butchered, Grandpa prepared tripe. The stomach of the animal is cleaned out, thoroughly washed and scrubbed. Grandpa used lye and water to cleanse and sterilize the stomach. The first step is to open and clean the stomach of all food materials, scraping and washing in cold water. Wash the stomach through several boiling waters, then put it in cold water and let it soak all night. After repeatedly boiling, scrape the tripe with a dull knife or scraper.

Tripe has a very small honey comb like composition. With the thoroughly cleaned **tripe cut in 3 to 5 inch pieces,** Mamma would dip it into **flour** seasoned with **salt** and **pepper,** and fry in **medium hot shortening** until crispy brown on both sides. This is really quite edible, and gives variety to the menu. Grandpa thoroughly enjoyed it, so we had tripe every winter.

Tripe for frying was rubbed on both sides with salt and kept in a cold place until needed. It was then soaked in cold water to remove the salt. Sometimes the water would have to be changed several times. Tripe can be parboiled to remove the salt. Place it in cold water, bring to boil for 3 to 4 minutes. Then pour off the water and repeat the process. This should remove enough salt so that the tripe is ready for use. If not, parboil again.

PICKLED TRIPE

Mamma pickled some of the tripe. She would fill a gallon stone jar 3/4 full with strips and cover it with a hot spice and vinegar solution. Use **5 cups of vinegar** and **3 cups water**, a **cup of sugar, two tablespoons of salt**, and **1 teaspoon of black pepper**. Bring to a boil and pour over the tripe. Hold down the meat with a plate and a clean, smooth rock and cover the jar with a heavy cloth or lid.

There are other methods of cooking tripe, but these are the ones preferred by Grandpa.

SCRAMBLED EGGS AND BRAINS

Another dish that Grandpa liked very much was scrambled eggs and brains. This is supposed to be a dish for an epicure and I guess Grandpa was an epicure, for he had eaten Grandma's cooking and then Mamma's.

Wash the brains carefully to remove all blood and any bits of bloody tissue. Use **2 tablespoons of butter** or **bacon fryings** and heat to medium hot in a **8" or 9" skillet**. Take **1 cup of brains and 2 eggs** and stir and turn, cooking until the eggs, both whites and yolks are firm. Sprinkle with **salt** and **pepper**.

HASH

In spite of the fact that "hash" is traditionally disparged, we liked hash.

It is cheap, it is easy to make, and it tastes good — very good.

Mamma used food to the last scrap, and boiled or roasted beef pieces sometimes were ground for hash.

Four cups of ground beef, firmly packed and **2 cups diced boiled potatoes** are added to **4 cups of beef broth** or **water**. Stir in **3 tablespoons butter, ½ teaspoon black pepper, 1 teaspoon sage** and **1 teaspoon salt**. If you use water, add 2 teaspoons bouillon and not as much salt.

Hash should be very moist, but not runny. Add more moisture if the hash is dry. Simmer for 15 minutes and serve hot.

The seasonings are all relative to your family's taste. It should have a distinct sage taste, but I have found that some cans of sage are very strong, so be careful or you may have too much sage. If you like it, a **small diced onion** may be added to the cooking potatoes.

I prefer hash on a chilly, rainy day, or perhaps a cold winter evening.

BAKED OR FRIED HASH

Baked hash is also good. After mixing all the materials, put it in a baking dish and bake until brown. This will not take as much liquid as boiled hash.

Either boiled, baked or fried hash is delicious, and it contains a vegetable as well as your meat. Bake buttermilk biscuits, open a can of chow-chow and a glass of buffalo berry jelly, and serve dried apple sauce or fresh apples stewed either with the hash or to finish off the meal.

If you want fried hash, use the ground meat and potatoes as already indicated, but use just enough liquid to moisten the meat. Heat 4 tablespoons lard in a skillet and when hot, add the meat and potatoes. As the hash browns, turn and stir until well browned.

THE LONG WINTER

A sharp, frosty morning, but a warming mid-day — that gradually became ominously still. The cattle came down the long lane from the pasture and turned their backs to the great blue-black clouds that came swirling from the north. Intermittent snowflakes drifted toward the brown prairies — then a few more. The howling winds tore at the barn, the shack — and all living things. A great wall of snow rushed across the plains, blotting out all signs of life, as the blizzard hurtled in.

So began the long winter.

BEAN SOUP AND COLD BISCUITS

Mamma was a teacher, a home maker, a feeder of chickens, caretaker of two or three cows and horses, and a hauler of water from the spring and grain to the elevator in Culbertson. When we first moved to Montana there were no available well-drilling machines, and since few of the shovel-dug wells produced water, it was hauled in barrels either on a stone boat or a wagon depending on the season of the year.

Bean soup for Saturday dinner became a traditional as well as logical dish for it was so easy to make. I am sure that no bean soup is as good as that made in an iron pot on an old coal stove — not even the bean soup for the Senators. I remember almost with nostalgia those bean soup dinners on the homestead.

Several variations can be used to season the soup, but just plain bean soup seasoned with bacon grease was a feast.

Following is the basic soup for eight to ten servings. Carefully sort **3 cups of navy beans** watching for tiny chunks of hard dirt, tiny pebbles, and worm holes. Wash thoroughly and put aside to soak overnight in three quarts of water. In the morning, place the pot of beans on the back of the stove and slowly simmer until soft and mealy. More water may have to be added, because of evaporation.

When the beans are nearly done, add **salt, pepper and bacon grease** (3 or 4 tablespoons) to taste. We usually had big, hard soda crackers, twice as big as the crackers of today, but not nearly as good as the modern version. I really enjoyed buttering generously both halves of a cold biscuit which I placed, butter side down, to soak in the hot soup. I also added fresh diced onions to my bowl of soup. Delicious!

Sometimes the recipe was varied by adding **diced bacon** or **salt pork** to the simmering beans. A very special variation was to use a **ham bone** with many pieces of ham clinging to the bone. These bits of ham, when well cooked, were a savory addition to the beans. Occasionally, **diced potatoes** were added half an hour before the soup was served.

A **teaspoon of ginger** or **half a teaspoon of soda** as a seasoning for the beans supposedly prevented gas formation. It may or may not help the gas situation but the ginger adds to the flavor of the beans.

CORN MEAL MUSH

When the thermometer did not drop too low, Olive and I played outside until the sun went down. We came in cold, tired, hungry, but happy. We peeled off our outdoor clothing layer by layer.

It was wonderful to sit down to a bowl of steaming hot mush, seasoned with sugar and milk. The heat of the kitchen stove and the hot mush would soon make us comfortably warm.

We didn't always use milk on the mush, but would season it with a big teaspoon of butter and a generous amount of brown sugar. The butter melted and dribbled down through the sugar and over the mush making a most appetizing dish. We might go back a second time and sometimes a third for another serving of that golden mush.

To make the mush, thoroughly mix **2 cups of yellow corn meal** and **3 teaspoons salt** into **2 cups of cold water**. Stir this mixture into **6 cups boiling water** and return to boil. Turn the heat down so the mush continues boiling slowly, and stir constantly. Cook at least 10 minutes or more in a **6 to 8 quart kettle**, stirring constantly with a big mixing spoon with long handle because the thick mush will plop up in big bubbles and may easily burn your hand. I sometimes use a kitchen mitten or wrap a small towel around my hand.

Sometimes we would have frozen apples to eat for dessert. If the afternoon had been very cold, we put a washed apple apiece out in the cold to freeze. When it froze solid, we took a dull kitchen knife or the side of a sharp kitchen spoon, and made curled shavings from the frozen apple. That was really good! Practically apple ice cream!

Mamma put the leftover mush into a square or oblong pan, three or four inches deep, pressed it down firmly and let stand for several hours or overnight. That was for fried mush.

If you really like fried mush, you should make a batch and a half of the mush or maybe a double batch so there will be plenty to fry.

The darkness came early on the prairies in winter time. After we had our supper and the dishes were washed, Mamma read to us, then off to bed we went — at 6 p.m. Once in a great while, coaxing would get us one more story, but generally the deadline was 6 p.m.

FRIED MUSH

If mush has been the supper dish, we have fried mush for breakfast. Cut the cold mush into slices nearly ½ inch thick and fry in two or three tablespoons of hot shortening until quite brown. You may have to add more shortening while cooking. It would be better to use 2 skillets for the frying mush as it browns very slowly.

I like the delicious crunchy nutlike flavor of the fried mush, just as it comes from the skillet, but some like it with syrup, or honey or jelly. It makes an excellent breakfast with just fruit. Fry bacon and eggs and you have a feast.

SCRAPPLE

Scrapple is made of mush (corn meal or some other cereal) and meat scraps. The hogs head, after it has been cleaned, may be boiled in slightly salted water until very, very tender. Take all the meat from the bones, dice any of the larger pieces and place in a large kettle.

Now use the regulation mush recipe doubled or tripled, and cook the pieces of pork with the mush. When done, place the combination in square or oblong pans, and allow to stand until thoroughly chilled. When chilled remove from pans, wrap for freezing and you will have scrapple on hand for several weeks.

Slice, cook, and serve the scrapple like fried mush, and it makes a very good breakfast or supper dish. Another way to make scrapple is to add crushed cracklings after lard making to the cooking mush. Bits of bacon or ham in the mush also makes a tasty scrapple.

SKIERS GO TO COAL BANK COULEE

Some Sundays the entire family went to Coal Bank Coulee. The coulee had fairly high steep hills, higher than any other hills near us. Several of the homesteaders had immigrated from Norway, and had been expert or champion skiers and jumpers in the old country. When the snow got deep, they would make ski slides or runs over the hills, and also a ski jump. Of course, the hills weren't nearly as high as in Norway, but they had a lot of fun and neighbors would come for miles to watch, and sometimes try their luck.

The tight suits and bright caps and scarves of the skiers, the frost-coated horses and blanket-filled sleds made a colorful picture against the snow-coated hills.

Some of the men would come off the jump, turn a somersault, land near the bottom of the hill in a crouching position, then ski off. I shivered from cold and also shivered clear down to my toes whenever they would jump and do that flip-flop.

The Norwegians liked their coffee and the smell of coffee wafted across the snow and smelled so good. We didn't have any coffee for Mamma didn't drink coffee and didn't allow Olive and me to drink it either.

Grandpa had his coffee. I ground it every morning. The coffee beans went into the cup of the grinder and I ground and ground. The ground coffee would drop into a little drawer. Mamma measured the coffee into a grey enameled coffee pot. When the coffee boiled, she set the pot on the back of the stove, and poured in half a cup of cold water to settle the grounds. The coffee stood a few minutes then was ready to pour. The pot stood on the back of the stove all day and Grandpa had coffee whenever he wanted it.

Olive and I liked pancakes very much, so when we returned from watching the skiers in Coal Bank Coulee, Mamma made pancakes.

The kitchen fire had been banked while we were gone. The damper was turned on and a quick shake of the grates and the fire began to burn briskly.

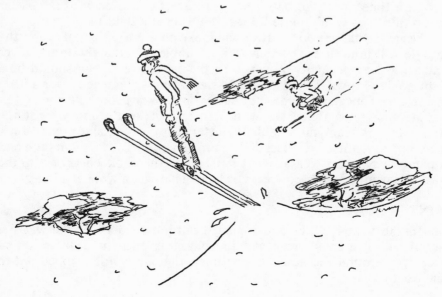

PANCAKES

Mamma put bacon in a big iron skillet to fry slowly on the back of the stove, as she stirred up the pancakes. The following recipe serves four people if they aren't too hungry.

Beat **2 eggs** until fluffy in a **4 quart mixing bowl.** Add **½ teaspoon salt, 1 tablespoon sugar, 3 tablespoons of fryings from bacon, 1½ cups of buttermilk** and stir. Thoroughly beat in **2 scant cups flour,** finally add **½ teaspoon soda** and **2 teaspoons baking powder** and mix well. (If you do not have buttermilk, use sweet milk, omit the soda and use 3 teaspoons of baking powder instead of two.) Spoon a tablespoon of bacon fryings into an iron griddle or big skillet. Heat to medium and spoon in the pancake dough. (The pancake batter has a consistency much like white Karo Syrup. If it is too thick, slowly add more milk, ¼ cup at a time, until the batter has the correct consistency. If the batter is too thin, slowly add more flour just a little at a time.)

Usually 3 tablespoons batter will make an average size cake, and the griddle will hold three at a time. When bubbles rise thickly on the cakes and the edges begin to brown, turn the cakes over. They should be a light golden brown. I used a flexible steel blade knife when I was a little girl to turn pancakes. We did not have a spatula or pancake turner.

Mamma fried the cakes while the rest of us ate and we got the pancakes hot from the griddle. I buttered my cakes, and poured on a generous amount of chokecherry syrup. There was always sorghum and a pancake syrup as well as jelly, but I liked the chokecherry syrup the best. We would have bacon, eggs or ham. That was a wonderful meal.

WINTER FUN

In the winter, Olive and I played outdoors whenever the weather permitted. The snow came and the blizzards piled hard drifts several feet deep around the house. Sometimes, these long drifts sloped out to the pasture.

We bundled up in many layers of clothes and went sliding or skiing. We wore long underwear, long black stockings, and black button or lace shoes. We wore black sateen bloomers that could be pulled below the knees, two petticoats — one outing flannel with long sleeves, the other black sateen, a wool dress, a long sleeved apron, a sweater, a coat, stocking caps and scarves or fascinators, long black leggings that button on the side plus high buckled overshoes, and mittens. Aunt Ella crochetted these beautiful red mittens for us.

Grandpa made us sleds with curved wooden runners, and could those sleds go! We had many a fast ride down the steep drifts. Sometimes we might take a spill and rub our faces in the icy, rough snow. That wasn't fun — but we always got up and tried again.

Other times, we tried skiing on home made skiis, made by shaping the end of strong narrow boards to resemble the points of real skiis. The points were soaked in a tub of water two or three days, then bent up and tied in position to dry. A short strap was nailed on each side of the skiis, making a loop for the foot to fit into. They certainly were not professional, but they gave us hours of fun as we played on the drifts. Sometimes, we used old barrel staves as skiis — they made an erratic track, but they were exciting to use, too.

We had so much fun, we hated to go in, but when we got just so cold, we went into the house and peeled off some of the outer layers of clothing and stood and turned by the great stove in the front room until we were warm. We bundled up again and went to play until we were cold once more.

It was wonderful to come in from the sometimes below zero cold, warm up and then have a baked bean dinner.

BAKED BEANS

There would always be a fire in the kitchen stove on chilly days in fall and winter. Mamma put beans to soak the night before and in the morning she put a ham bone or cured pig hocks in the bean pot and cooked the beans and meat slowly for an hour or two.

Two cups of dried beans covered with **six cups of water** and simmered until almost all the water is gone, will make approximately six cups of cooked beans.

Place the **six cups of boiled beans** in a **deep baking dish** or casserole, (iron pot if you have one) shred or dice the **ham**, add **1 medium size diced onion**, flavor with **2 to 6 tablespoons of catsup** and the same amount of **brown sugar**. Season with **salt** and **½ teaspoon black pepper**. (Keep enough moisture on the beans, so they will not become dry and hard.) Bake slowly and stir occasionally. They are baked for at least one hour or an hour and a half or until well done.

When the beans start baking, scrub some large potatoes and put them in the oven, too. Stir up a batch of corn bread, turn the oven to hot, and begin baking 30 minutes before dinner. When ready to bake the corn bread, remove beans from oven and allow to simmer slowly on stove. If the potatoes are done, also take from oven and keep in a warm place.

Serve cold cabbage or cole slaw for a salad. This makes a good nutritious meal that sticks to the ribs on a cold day! If a person is still hungry and wants more food — a fresh apple makes an excellent dessert.

LIMA BEANS OR BUTTER BEANS

I always enjoyed Mamma's butter beans, but it seemed to me that Cousin Lillie cooked the best ones.

The beans were always big, and were cooked until they were tender, but did not fall to pieces.

After the beans were tender, Cousin Lillie added cream or rich milk, salt and pepper, butter and thickener. They would just melt in the mouth.

Cover **2 cups of the large lima beans**, with **5 cups cold water** and soak overnight. Bring to boil and simmer for one hour or until tender. This may take another hour depending upon the altitude and humidity of the air. I find that some beans take much longer to cook than others. This may be the variety of the bean or they may be older, and therefore are dryer. The beans are cooked tightly covered in a small amount of water. It may be necessary to add water occasionally. When the butter beans are tender, add **2 cups of milk, 2 tablespoons butter**, and **thickener**. Bring to a boil, then simmer slowly until thick. They are good served as a vegetable or as a substitute for meat, as they are high in protein.

BUTTER BEANS AND SHORT RIBS

While the beans are cooking, bake 2 pounds of short ribs until almost tender. When both the beans and short ribs are nearly done, place the short ribs in a large casserole, cover with the beans, and bake until completely tender. Serve with cole slaw and a dish of fruit. Corn bread is good with this dinner.

BOILED DINNER

Coal Bank Coulee was not far from Cousin Lillie's homestead, and in the fall, Grandpa would haul enough coal (a soft lignite) from this mine to do for the winter. The first year or two, Grandpa had no difficulty in unloading the coal, but gradually Mamma or Elsie or perhaps, both of them did the unloading and finally they had to do the hauling.

Olive and I helped by throwing some coal in the window, a lump at a time or some on a small shovel. If any of the Uncles were there, of course they took over. If Mamma hauled the coal, I cooked dinner. A hearty boiled dinner was wonderful on a frosty fall or winter day.

Early in the morning, Mamma put a **3 or 4 pound piece of boiling beef** with **6 to 8 cups of water** in a large pot on the back of the stove to simmer. When time for dinner was nearing, Grandpa built up the kitchen fire. I peeled and quartered **1 medium size potato** for each member of the family plus 2 or 3 extra potatoes, and did the same with **carrots** and **turnips.** I put **several small onions** into the pot and cut a **medium** or **large head of cabbage** into 8 sections, leaving part of the core in each section to hold the cabbage leaves together.

About the middle of the morning, I added a scant **tablespoon of salt** to the boiling beef and maybe some more water. When time to cook the vegetables arrived, I took out 3 or 4 cups of the beef soup and put the potatoes, carrots, onions, and turnips around the meat. I placed the cabbage sections on top of the meat and other vegetables, then poured the soup over the cabbage for seasoning, covered the kettle tightly, and pulled it forward to a hotter spot on the stove.

I made buttermilk biscuits and by time the biscuits baked, dinner was ready. Olive set the table and if Mamma was very late, Grandpa, Olive and I went ahead and ate our dinners.

When Mamma came in cold, tired and hungry, she was very glad to sit down and eat. She didn't drink coffee, but sometimes she made a cup of green tea to go with her dinner if she were very cold. Sometimes other sleds or wagons had reached the coal bank before she did, and she waited for hours for her load of coal.

My family all like boiled dinners, and we have it several times during the winter months. I always put in extra vegetables. It is good warmed up, just as it is.

BEEF STEW

The **vegetables** and **meat** may be diced in rather large chunks, then add **cans of tomatoes, corn,** and **beans.** Simmer for half an hour for a tasty stew.

A boil or stew may be served with crackers or hot or cold buttermilk biscuits.

Beet relish or beet pickles add color to the tablesetting. A dish of stewed dried apricots makes a good dessert.

OTHER STEWS

Other stew ideas are as follows: — The basic for a stew is meat, but just a combination of vegetables and broth or bouillon and butter is very satisfactory.

I keep any dabs of left over cooked vegetables in the freezing compartment of the refrigerator. There may be potatoes, green beans, peas, carrots, corn, lima beans, red kidney beans, tomatoes, celery, rice, cabbage, onions or what have you, in either the refrigerator or freezer. Sometimes I put everything in the stew, and again only three or four vegetables. I like diced beef chunks and broth as the base, but bologna or weiners cut in small chunks, with bouillon, hot water and butter plus three or four vegetables is quite edible. Salt and pepper to taste.

If I have a yen for stew and not enough cooked vegetables on hand, I use my small pressure cooker, dice some raw vegetables, and very soon there will be a good meal.

I like a stew with only a small amount of soup or liquid.

OLIVE AND I GO FOR A WALK

I was an avid reader of the Elsie Dinsmore books. The heroine, Elsie Dinsmore, was always going for a walk, so I decided to go for a walk. It didn't make any difference to me that Elsie Dinsmore lived in the South and that it was February in Montana. Olive and I bundled up to go out to play and then took off.

We went out into the big pasture and over toward the spring in a coulee nearly a mile away. It was a beautiful, sunny day, but cold! We never noticed the cold at first. Drifts of snow were packed and hard, so we walked the crusty surface, but occasionally we broke through. Then the snow went under our dresses and worked down into the top of our leggings and into our mittens. Gradually the cold began to seep through our clothes.

We must have wandered nearly a mile. The sun dipped down in the west, and a slight breeze began to blow. We decided we had walked enough, and couldn't understand why Elsie Dinsmore took so many walks. That return home took a very, very long time. We went back a different way and kept breaking through the snow, getting colder and colder. By the time we reached home, we ached so with the cold, we just stumbled along.

Olive's face was red and tears were frozen around her eyes. I know I was crying some, and my face burned and stung from the cold.

Mamma was ironing, but suddenly realized we had been outside a long time. She called us, and there was no answer. She had wrapped up and was just going to look for us, when we stumbled in.

We were so cold, Mamma and Grandpa helped us take off our outdoor clothes and then we sat shaking huddled by the big stove. As the heat permeated, our feet and hands began to ache — and my chilblain began to hurt. I always had chilblain from the first frost in the fall, until spring arrived.

Mamma made some tomato soup and that hot, rosy-colored soup with chunks of tomatoes floating in it, was the most delicious soup I ever ate.

Mamma didn't even scold us, for we very quickly assured her that we would *never, never* take another walk.

TOMATO SOUP

Pour **3 cups of stewed or canned tomatoes** (not strained) into a **6 quart kettle**. Bring to a boil, and simmer for 5 minutes. Add **1 scant teaspoon soda**. The tomatoes will fiz up, and when they quit fizzing, add **4 to 6 cups of milk, 2 to 4 tablespoons of butter, a teaspoon of salt** and **¼ teaspoon of black pepper**.

Bring to boiling point and serve. Tomato soup is very tasty with crackers, and also is very satisfying.

CHRISTMAS ON THE HOMESTEAD

Christmas was a wonderful day on the prairies. We began studying the toy pages in the Sears, Roebuck Catalog early in the fall when the winter catalog arrived. Olive and I exchanged gifts with our cousins, James and Violet, picking out the gifts we wanted and changing our minds many times until the family order went in to Sears sometime in November. The order was large and included family Christmas presents, food and clothing. There might be long warm underwear, heavy stockings, sweaters, stocking caps, and sometimes a new coat. But it included packages of "Soft A" sugar, raisins, currants, dates, canned fish, dried apples, apricots, and pears, hard candies, ribbon candy, stick candy, English walnuts, filberts, brazil nuts and other hard to get food items. When the boxes arrived, Mamma always carefully put some things away, so we knew they were Christmas presents for us — always books, maybe a toy or game, and occasionally a new doll.

We made the money for the family presents we ordered by trapping gophers — a penny for each gopher caught. We wrapped and unwrapped the presents that we got for each other so many times before Christmas, we nearly wore them out, but that was part of the fun.

It seemed very important to us that December 21 was the shortest day in the year for Christmas day would be just a little bit longer and those extra moments were precious.

Greenery was scarce on the prairies, but the house was decorated with some small ground junipers found in the coulees.

One year we were both excited and overwhelmed by the arrival of Uncle John from North Dakota just before Christmas. The high-light of his arrival was that he brought a Christmas tree from Culbertson.

I don't think there was ever a more beautiful tree. Olive and I were so excited that we got up every time the clock struck the hour — rather we tried to get up to see our Christmas presents and the tree, but Mamma always managed to get us back into bed before we reached the tree. Finally, about three o'clock, we were fast asleep and didn't wake up until Mamma called us for breakfast. We felt quite deflated and Uncle John teased us all day.

All of the relatives gathered at Grandpa's for that Christmas dinner. We had roast chicken and baked dressing, mashed potatoes and gravy, candied yams (from a can), canned corn, slaw, celery, cranberries, mixed pickles, pear pickles, jelly, light bread biscuits, mincemeat pie, fruit cake, white cake, snow cream, and ambrosia.

After dinner was over and the dishes washed, Mamma brought out her delicious homemade candy — pink coconut creams, taffy, chocolate drops, and neapolitan. The neapolitan had four layers — chocolate, pink, yellow, and white fondant, with chopped nuts worked into the fondant. The neapolitan candy was my favorite: I held small bites in my mouth as the combination of lemon, vanilla, and chocolate slowly melted, then I chewed up the nuts. I make good neapolitan candy, but nothing compared to those memories of Mamma's candy on the prairie.

Mamma would only give us nibbles of candy before the holidays as she wanted to save the candy for Christmas. I remember one Christmas morning, I slipped quietly out of bed, while it was still dark, and got into the candy and Olive and I enjoyed a piece of each kind in bed. Mamma was quite exasperated, but I said very innocently "You said we could have some on Christmas day." I wasn't punished that time, I guess because it was Christmas, but Mamma was usually very strict with us, if we overstepped a fraction of an inch.

Several persons were invited to these special dinners, so everybody couldn't eat at the table at one time. Mamma cleaned up and set the table three times. The children ate at the third table. We became desperately hungry, for it seemed to take the grown-ups hours to eat, talk, exchange news and laugh. There was plenty of food, but the long wait was so difficult.

ROAST OR BAKED CHICKEN

For the first few years on the prairies, baked or roasted chicken was the meat dish for our traditional Thanksgiving and Christmas dinners. We didn't go to a butcher shop to get our chickens either. A couple of days before Christmas, we went to the barnyard or chicken house and caught the chickens.

They were then beheaded, by either a sharp ax or by wringing the neck. Before beheading, the wings were crossed in back. They couldn't flop around as much and splatter blood. They were held up and allowed to bleed a short time and then dunked in a large kettle of boiling water. Mamma held the feet with a firm grip. The chicken was plunged in and out of the water, and swirled around in the water, getting every feather well soaked.

Now Olive and I took over. We pulled out all the feathers and the pin feathers, the big wing and tail feathers first. (Pinfeathers are the beginning of new feathers, sometimes the tips extend beyond the skin and sometimes are merely dark splotches.) We had to get them all out, sometimes it was very hard to pull them. We even had to take pliers and pull hard. On an older bird, wing and tail feathers were difficult. After the chicken was defeathered, Mamma singed it. She rolled one end of a newspaper very tightly and the other end was fluted out like a horn. She lighted the loose end of the paper and while holding the chicken first by a leg and then by the wing, singed off all the hairs. She finished the job by thoroughly washing and dressing or drawing the bird. We were especially interested in watching the cleaning of the gizzard, and the removal of the gall-bladder from the liver. It was also fun to hear the windpipe come out with a big plop.

By 9 a.m. Christmas morning, the chickens were in the oven.

Mamma had a long bread pan that would hold two chickens side by side — the breasts up. Mamma rubbed **butter** generously over the breast, legs and wings, sprinkled **flour** over the butter, and then scattered **1 teaspoon of salt** over each chicken. She poured **6 or 7 cups of water** in the bottom of the pan, and as the chicken cooked more water would be added to replace loss by evaporation.

When the flour and meat had browned, the chickens were turned over, and **butter, salt and flour** were added. After the back was browned, the chicken was turned again, and more flour sprinkled on. This time, as the browning process continued, Mamma basted the chicken. She would use a big spoon and dip broth from the pan and pour over the exposed parts. This kept the roast from burning and kept it moist and tender. The basting and turning of the chicken continued until it was tender, juicy, and mouth-watering. The well-seasoned liquid was drained off into a big bowl, and divided for the baked dressing and the gravy.

The baking pan was covered and placed on the back of the range to keep the meat warm. The **bread, onions, sage, salt** and **pepper** were ready for the liquid which was now added and the mixture stirred, then poured into a pan for the baked dressing.

— If there was not enough liquid from around the chickens to soften the bread — hot water and butter were added. Today, if I don't have enough liquid or broth I use hot water, butter, and bouillon. (One teaspoon of bouillon and one cup water.)

— If you want dressing and do not have any broth, just use the hot water, bouillon and butter. It isn't quite as good as the real broth — but still makes a very tasty substitute.

GRAVY

The remaining liquid is used for the gravy. It is rich and tasty and there may be enough flour from basting the chicken to make it thick enough. If not, make a thickener of water and flour in a pint jar. Heat the broth to the boiling point and slowly pour in the thickener a little at a time stirring constantly until the gravy has the consistency you want. You may have to add some salt and pepper, but that depends on the cook's taste.

INDIANA TRADITION — "YAMS"

Fresh yam and sweet potatoes were not available for the Christmas dinner, so canned yams were used, since Christmas dinner was not Christmas dinner without candied yams.

Mamma would put a layer of **yams** in a **deep crock** or **baking pan**, **butter** generously, cover also generously with **brown sugar**, then would come another layer of yams, butter and brown sugar, until she had used two cans of the deep gold yams in the baking dish. All yam eaters declared that this was a savory dish.

CORN

Corn is easy to fix. Just open **2 regular cans of corn**, and it can be either creamed or buttered. If you want creamed corn, boil the corn until it is almost dry, add **2 cups of milk** and **4 tablespoons butter**. Bring to boil and gradually stir in thickener made by shaking **4 tablespoons of flour** in **halfcup of cold water** in a covered pint jar.

Stir constantly until the milk has thickened; a small amount of salt and pepper may be added. The corn is ready to serve.

COLE SLAW

Cabbage slaw or cole slaw or just slaw as far as I am concerned, is a Christmas must. That is what it was when I was young and that is what it is now that I am older.

I use a grater and cut the cabbage, but none of that for Mamma. She carefully sharpened her best knife on an old crock or whetstone and got out her cutting board. She selected a solid head of cabbage, cut off excess leaves and cut the head in half. Then she cut down through the cabbage making very fine strips or shavings. (I never could cut the cabbage that fine, and it was so tedious to try.) After getting a pile of the cabbage, she would then cut across it, making it just as fine the other way. I will admit the texture of that shredded cabbage was excellent for slaw.

Pour a **quart** of the **cut cabbage** into a **mixing bowl.** Have the following dressing already prepared and chilled.

BASIC VINEGAR DRESSING

Place **¼ cup of vinegar** and **¼ cup of water** in a **pint kettle.** Add **4 tablespoons butter, 4 tablespoons sugar** and bring to a boil, stirring constantly. Allow to cool before putting on cabbage. Sprinkle **½ teaspoon of salt** and **¼ teaspoon pepper** on the cabbage and add the dressing. The slaw may be served from a serving dish or you may use individual salad dishes. If it is a home style meal, let each person serve himself.

Some vinegars are very strong and a person just doesn't know which bottle will be strong until you try it. If a particular bottle is very strong, cut down on the amount of vinegar but add enough water to make the ½ cup. Some individuals prefer their salad less sweet, so cut down on the amount of sugar, if you are in that group.

Four tablespoons make one-fourth cup of liquid or solids, so if you measure by tablespoons you may find it easier to adjust the amounts of the ingredients for variants in taste.

CHRISTMAS BAKING

The Christmas fruit cake was baked before Thanksgiving. It seemed that the Thanksgiving and Christmas seasons blended into a continuous aroma of tempting foods. The spiciness of the fruit cake lingered in the house for days — cinnamon, allspice, cloves, citron, currants, and raisins.

CHRISTMAS FRUIT CAKE

Cream **1 cup of sugar** with **1 cup of butter.** Add **½ cup of sorghum molasses** with **1 teaspoon of soda.** Beat **7 egg yolks** and stir well into the above mixture.

Put **½ pound citron, 1 pound raisins,** and **1 pound currants** into a **large mixing bowl.** Sprinkle **½ cup of sifted flour** over the fruit and mix or dredge well. This prevents the fruit from sinking to the bottom of the cake pan while cake is baking.

Add **1 tablespoon of vanilla** to the butter, sugar, yolks, and molasses mixture. Spices came next — **1 tablespoon cinnamon, 1 tablespoon nutmeg, ½ tablespoon ground cloves.** Gradually stir in **3½ cups sifted flour** and beat well. Add the fruit and be sure that it is well mixed. Finally fold in the stiffly beaten **whites of the seven eggs,** and fold or stir just enough to mix.

Grease **two 7" x 10" x 3" pans** well and put two or three layers of **waxed paper** on the bottom of the pan. Grease the top layer of paper and shake a little flour into the cake pan. Keep turning and twisting the pan until the paper and sides of the pan are completely covered by a very thin coating of flour.

Pour an equal amount of batter into each pan and spread outward from the center of the pan. If the batter is lower in the center of the pan, the cake will be level when cooked.

Place the fruit cake in a 300° oven and bake for 2½ hours, or until done. At 2 hours start testing for doneness by inserting a toothpick into the cake. When the toothpick comes out clean — the cake is done. When the cakes come from the oven, the crusts are a shiny reddish brown splashed with chewy raisins and currants.

(But Mamma would not allow us to have even one little taste.)

Set the pans on a cake rack and when cool, turn out on a cloth covered bread board, remove the paper, and allow to get entirely cold.

When cold, wrap the cake in a cloth dampened in apple juice, apple cider, or if you prefer a small amount of brandy. Next, wrap it in waxed paper, and finally in a heavy cloth or towel. Mamma stored the cakes in a tin bread box, placed in a very cold dark place to "ripen."

It was quite an important occasion when the cake was finally cut five or six weeks later. A sharp knife cut one very thin slice for each of us. Mamma critically examined the texture as we wiggled in excitement. We ate that dark rich cake almost ceremoniously. Was it as good as the cake last year? To me, each cake always tasted better than the one of the year before.

We savored those thin slices of Christmas cake to the last currant and crumb and looked hopefully for just another bite — but the cake had to be saved for Christmas and for company.

JEAN'S FRUIT CAKE

Here is another excellent fruit cake. The recipe for this cake is not as old as Mamma's fruit cake, but is, nevertheless, a homesteader cake. My Cousin Jean MacLeod — Uncle Bert and Aunt Hattie's daughter — gave me this recipe. It is delicious, and it can be used immediately, for it does not go through a ripening state.

Cream **1 cup of shortening** with **3 cups sugar**. Add **2 large or 3 small eggs**, slightly beaten, and **1 tablespoon lemon extract**. Beat thoroughly three or four minutes. Add **3 cups unsweetened apple sauce** and beat three more minutes. Alternate mixing **1 cup boiling water** and **4 teaspoons of soda** with **4½ cups sifted flour** and stir into the above mixture, about 1 cup at a time. Now add **1 teaspoon salt, 1 teaspoon cinnamon, ½ teaspoon cloves**, and **½ teaspoon allspice**, and mix. Lastly put **2 cups raisins, 1 cup chopped nuts**, and **2 cups candied fruit** into a **mixing bowl** and coat with **½ cup of flour**. Add this fruit, nut and flour mixture to the cake and stir in thoroughly.

Have the oven heated to 300°. Grease **two 12" x 16" bread pans**, put in a layer of wax paper, grease and flour wax paper, and pour half the mixture into each pan.

Cook for 1 hour and 20 minutes to 30 minutes. The cake is done when an inserted toothpick comes out clean, or the cake, when touched lightly on top with a finger, will come back into place.

When the cakes are cold, cut into easily handled squares, wrap and freeze. Of course, don't forget to give the family generous samples before you store for special occasions.

Comments — This recipe will be all right baked in one large pan (2 pound size) and 5 small ones (1 pound).

— Fruit cakes are lovely for presents for non-cooking friends and relatives. Decorate the top of the individual cake with sliced **green** and **red candied pineapple** and either **pecan** or **walnut halves**. Wrap in clear plastic paper and tie with an attractive brightly colored bow.

MINCEMEAT

The rich smell of the cooking mincemeat with the spices, apples, raisins and currants filled the house and lingered for days reminding us constantly of the holiday festivities ahead. We were in a constant tingle of excitement.

Mamma made mincemeat after fall butchering. She used the

tougher cuts of meat — the neck, the shank, the brisket, or other bony pieces of beef. She cooked this meat slowly until very tender, so that it could be removed easily from the bone — Olive and I helped by grinding the meat with the food chopper.

To make 3 to 4 quarts mincemeat:

Place **4 cups ground meat, 8 cups chunky apple sauce** (unsweetened) and **2 cups liquid** (see below) in a **6 quart kettle.** To this add: **5 cups brown sugar (packed), 2 cups butter*, ½ cup vinegar** (leave out vinegar if cider is used), **2 teaspoons cinnamon, ¼ teaspoon cloves, ¼ teaspoon allspice.**

If you wish, add the **juice of 1 lemon** and **1 orange.** Beef broth or apple juice or cider, or water may be used for the liquid. Mix the ingredients and simmer for 45 minutes. You may have to add additional liquid as you cook the mincemeat, so it will not become too dry.

*Many old timers used suet instead of butter. If you wish to use suet, cook and grind enough suet to make 2 cups. Suet is the roll of pure fat found around the kidneys and loins of sheep or beef animals. I have found that if you use suet, the pie must be served hot, or the suet will be lumpy and will stick to your tongue, palate, and teeth (a very unpleasant sensation). I always use butter.

Mamma put the mincemeat in a stone jar and placed it in the pantry which was cold. It seemed to keep indefinitely.

I make only a small amount of mincemeat, in order to have pies for Thanksgiving and Christmas, and I keep it refrigerated until used.

If you make a large amount of mincemeat, put it in quart jars and process in the pressure cooker according to directions. Then it will keep indefinitely.

My children took their lunches to school, and John was especially fond of mincemeat sandwiches. They also came home from school and made mincemeat sandwiches for after school snacks.

I find a good quality of wild meat is good in mincemeat. In fact, I prefer it to beef as there is not as much fat or tallow in the tissues.

CHRISTMAS CANDIES

Mamma's Christmas candies were one of the highlights of the holiday season and I knew of no one at that time except members of the immediate family making neapolitan, coconut creams, lemon creams or chocolate drops. When we were small, we were seldom allowed to watch Mamma make candies. It was so hard to keep from saying "Please, just give me one bite," or ask to scrape the kettle or pan, even before Mamma was done with it.

Mamma much preferred that we would be in bed and asleep.

But we always knew when candy had been made, because we could still smell the sweet aroma the next morning, and we generally located the hiding place, although it was against the rules to eat any without permission until Christmas day. It was all a delightful part of the secrets of Christmas time.

FONDANT

Fondant is the basic requisite for neapolitan and the other cream candies. Good fondant is firm but creamy and has no grains or granules.

Follow directions carefully to attain this perfection. Place **2 cups white sugar, 1 tablespoon white Karo,** and **1 cup boiling water** in a **mixing bowl** and stir until sugar is entirely dissolved. Pour this mixture into a **2 or 3 quart kettle,** being careful that none of the mixture splashes up on the sides. Place on medium high heat and bring to a boil. If any sugar granules or moisture collects on the sides of the kettle, very carefully remove with a moistened paper towel. Boil the syrup until it forms a soft ball when dropped in a cup of cold water or a candy thermometer reaches 240°.

Begin to test for the soft ball stage in about six minutes. Carefully use a teaspoon and take a very small amount of the syrup and drop into ice cold water. The ball must be soft but firm enough to pick up. Texture is of prime importance in making good fondant. If the ball is so soft that it flattens quickly, the candy will not become firm enough to knead. If too firm, the fondant will be hard, lacking that desired soft, creamy consistency.

The best advice I am able to give is to experiment until you have actually worked with the fondant, it is difficult to know the right consistency.

The degrees on a candy thermometer is relative, because altitude, temperature of the kitchen and humidity all will affect the number of degrees. I have more confidence in the "soft-ball" method.

As soon as the fondant has reached the proper stage of doneness, pour it into a clean **4 quart mixing bowl,** and place the bowl into the pan of cold water. Allow to stand for a few minutes until the syrup has cooled. **Under no circumstances allow this syrup to be touched or moved.** If it is moved, the candy will probably be sugary.

When the syrup has cooled but still warm (about 5 minutes), quickly remove from the water at the same time beating with a large mixing spoon. Continue with the same motion and never stop beating until the fondant has formed. The syrup will gradually thicken and become milky in appearance. As you continue beating, the fondant will turn very thick and white, quickly becoming stiff enough to be kneaded and shaped with the hands. I refrigerate the fondant for several hours for efficient handling. Now the fondant is ready for the shaping into the various forms and types of candy.

On the homestead, Mamma only made fondant in the winter as we had no means of refrigeration.

NEAPOLITAN

Since neapolitan is my favorite of the fondant candies, I will explain how to make it first. You will need **four batches of the basic fondant recipe.** A double batch isn't difficult to make but if your arm tires easily, do not try it as you may become so tired that your fondant will not have the correct consistency.

In each fourth, make a deep dent with your fingers. In one part put a **few drops of yellow food coloring and 1 teaspoon lemon extract.** Knead this thoroughly until the flavor and color are entirely mixed. Leave one part white and add **vanilla flavoring.** Another part could be pink with **vanilla** or **orange flavoring.** Add **bitter chocolate** melted, **1 ounce,** or **2 or 3 tablespoons of cocoa** to the fourth part. Chocolate and cocoa are drying ingredients, so may thicken the fondant. If it does, add a drop or two at a time of hot water and knead into the mixture until the texture is the same consistency as the other fondant.

I put **¼ to ½ cup finely chopped walnuts or pecans** into each portion and work in smoothly. You are now ready to build your neapolitan.

Lightly spread **powdered sugar** on a **two foot length of waxed paper** on a large flat surface. Work the chocolate fondant into a long 2 inch wide ribbon approximately ½ inch thick. Dip a limber knife blade in water, shake and then smooth the top of the chocolate. Continue dipping and smoothing the chocolate fondant until the top is smooth and damp. This dampness helps bind the yellow fondant to the chocolate. Place the yellow fondant on the chocolate, using the same proportions, followed by the pink and then the white.

Use a long sharp kitchen knife, that has been dipped in cold water and holding the candy layers on one side with your hand, work along the other side with the side of knife — evening the layers as much as possible. Straighten the other side of the candy. Square off the sides and ends with the knife. Push the scraps aside until later.

You are now ready to cut the neapolitan block into 1/2 inch slices.

Cut crosswise through the layered block of candy and place the pieces on lightly buttered platters or waxed paper dusted with powdered sugar. You may have to dip your knife in hot water to make cutting easier.

Allow the finished product to stand for a few hours to slightly dry on surface, then store in airtight containers for Christmas. Separate each layer of candy with waxed paper.

The scraps that were pushed aside may be rolled into a long inch thick ribbon and sliced into ½ inch pieces, that may be eaten before Christmas. They are delicious as they have all the colors and flavor of the neapolitan, but in a marbleized instead of the layered design. Warning — keep the family out of the kitchen or all your scraps will disappear before they can be used.

CHOCOLATE DROPS

After basic fondant has stood tightly covered in a cold place or in the refrigerator for 2 or 3 days to ripen, form the shapes for the chocolate drops. The centers may be left white, or may be colored pink, yellow, light orange or pale green. I think vanilla, lemon, orange and mint extracts correspond to the colors. Use your imagination and shape the ripened fondant into round mounds, pointed mounds, squares, oblongs, or what have you. Finely chopped nuts worked into the fondant gives interesting variation.

After forming the fondant pieces for the chocolates, cover them tightly and return to refrigerator to chill thoroughly.

On the homestead we could not buy the commercial chocolate for dipping the fondant, so we used either **sweet** or bitter chocolate (according to taste preference) and used **1 ounce of parowax** for each **pound of chocolate.** The chocolate and parowax are grated and put in the top of a double boiler to melt. Keep the water at a lower boiling heat and stir the chocolate constantly while melting. If you wish your chocolates to have a shiny, dark look, keep the chocolate from overheating. Lower the heat until the water just barely simmers. If the chocolate spreads too much when the dipped chocolate is placed on a platter, add a small amount of melted parowax to the chocolate mixture.

Spread wax paper out on a flat surface ready for the dipped chocolates. Use a metal fork with fine tines, a pickle fork, a toothpick, or even a nut pick inserted into the fondant for dipping. The room temperature should be between 60° to 70°.

On the homestead, we had no difficulty keeping the room cool in the winter time. We would just allow the fire to go down, and the cold would come creeping in. Now I set the thermostat at 60° and the temperature will soon be cool enough.

We never make chocolates in the summer time, but if you feel compelled to, just place your table in front of the refrigerator and open the door. Of course, you will use more electricity, but it should take only a few minutes to dip two or three dozen chocolates. Setting the air conditioner also helps to lower the temperature.

The dipping process is as follows: dip the shaped fondant into the chocolate combination, swirl around, hold above the container for the excess chocolate to drip off, then place the chocolate on the wax paper. If it does not drop easily from the fork, push off with a tooth pick. Make a small chocolate design with a twist of your finger on top of the candy to give a professional look. You may wish to put half a pecan on your vanilla flavored candies or perhaps a half walnut or cashew nut on the lemon and orange flavored. I crack my own nuts when I want halves for decorative purposes.

While dipping the candies, occasionally stir the chocolate so the texture will remain smooth. If it thickens too much, slowly re-melt and return the fondant to the refrigerator to keep firm while doing so. Keep the water hot under the chocolate container.

After the candies are dipped, let them cool before moving while the chocolate sets. Store the chocolates in a covered container with waxed paper between layers of candies. I have found that they will keep for several days or even weeks.

You cannot taste the parowax in the chocolate, but there is a tendency for the chocolate to have a whitish look at times. Grocery stores sometimes have dipping chocolate on hand, and you may also purchase it from regular candy shops, where they make their own candy.

COCONUT CREAMS

I make coconut creams by mixing **1 cup of ground** or **flaked coconut** into a **pound of fondant.** Use either **lemon** or **vanilla extract** and **yellow** or **pink food coloring.** These coconut creams are an interesting and delicious method for giving variety to your candy making.

Small boxes that have been saved during the year, or boxes purchased at a novelty store, attractively decorated and wrapped, make welcome gifts for friends, relatives and shut-ins.

FUDGE

Fudge is an old favorite and practically everybody makes fudge successfully, to a more or less degree. Good fudge has a texture comparable to a good fondant — soft and smooth. If the weather was disagreeable, and we couldn't get outside to play, Olive and I would talk Elsie into making fudge, for she was the fudge-maker on the homestead. Here is Elsie's recipe.

Grate **2 squares unsweetened chocolate** and add **2 cups sugar, 2 tablespoons Karo or white corn syrup, 1 tablespoon butter** and **1 cup rich milk or ½ cup milk and ½ cream.** Cook slowly and stir to keep from scorching. With a damp cloth or paper towel, wipe the sides of the kettle to remove sugar granules. It may be necessary to do this three or four times. Cook the fudge to the soft ball stage. (By a soft ball, I mean a firm ball, that is soft but will not flatten.)

Pour into a **clean kettle, or mixing bowl,** and let stand for approximately 10 minutes. Add **1 teaspoon vanilla.** Beat until thick enough to pile into mounds. Sometimes it takes several minutes of beating, so if you do not have a strong arm and a great deal of patience, have somebody to "spell you." When the fudge stands in mounds pour onto a **buttered platter,** spread out, and cut into squares when cool.

Sometimes Elsie would make just plain fudge, sometimes she would **add chopped English Walnuts,** and sometimes **black walnuts.** That is, if

Olive and I would crack and pick out the walnuts. Olive and I felt the only trouble with the fudge making was that it didn't happen often enough.

— If rich milk or cream is not available, 1 cup of undiluted evaporated milk makes a good substitute.

CHRISTMAS ICE CREAM

An American tradition, home-made ice cream, is tops and its cold smoothness is a taste sensation not to be forgotten.

Sugared fresh blackberries, strawberries, or raspberries, used as toppings are really superb.

One year, all of the relatives of the community were having Christmas dinner at Grandpa's, and we were going to have ice cream. Enough cream had been saved, so we would have two gallon freezers full.

Mamma stirred up the mixture, took it over to Uncle Sid's to be frozen. All of the men took turns at the crank. Finally it became very hard to turn, so the extra water was poured off, more ice and salt packed around the ice cream can, and the freezer was set aside until the end of dinner.

I could hardly wait until the freezer was opened. But there was no ice cream that Christmas day. Salt had gotten into it. The freezer was an old one that had come from Indiana. No one had thought to check it, for at the last using it was all right. A hole had rusted through along the bottom seam of the can, and salt had leaked in from the brine. It was a very bitter disappointment, as we had talked about the ice cream we didn't have for days and days.

Later Grandpa soldered the hole in the ice cream can and we had many freezers full during homestead days.

Mamma usually made a custard as the basis for her ice cream, because it saved cream, and the texture was soft and smooth.

The following recipe will make two quarts of ice cream. If you plan to make a gallon, just double the recipe.

Mix **1½ cups milk, 3/4 cups of sugar** and **½ teaspoon salt** in the **top of a double boiler.** Beat **3 eggs** until quite frothy and stir into the milk. Cook in the top of the double boiler, stirring occasionally, until quite thick and smooth. Pour in **3 cups cream**, add **2 teaspoons vanilla.** Allow to stand until chilled. Never fill the freezer can more than 2/3 full, as the contents expands as it freezes.

Pour the custard into the freezer can, put in the dasher, and cover. Lower the can into the freezer. Put the crank on, fitting it over the top of the dasher, and lock in place. Put ice in a burlap bag and pound with a hammer until fine. Pour in layers of ice, and coarse salt until the bucket is full. (The salt lowers the temperature of the ice.)

Keep the crank turning steadily, if you want a smooth, creamy ice cream. Be careful as the ice melts, or salty water may go under the lid into the ice cream. A sheet of wax paper under the lid should prevent this from happening. As the water melts, pour it off, and add more ice and salt around the ice cream can.

When the crank becomes very hard to turn, take the top off carefully, pull out the dasher, pushing back the ice cream with a big spoon, but don't push back too much. The children will want to scrape the dasher. Put it in a big pan and turn them loose with spoons.

Put the cover back on the freezer can. Cover with a heavy clean cloth. Pack the freezer with ice and salt and put in a cool place until time to serve.

APPLE BOXES MAKE OUR TABLE

Mamma taught school one fall up on Antelope Creek. Pupils ranged in age from five years to twenty-three in all the elementary eight grades. I was seven at the time, and in the second grade. The older pupils were very engrossed in their own affairs, but still were considerate of the little ones.

One weekend, Pearl Rice, one of the big girls, invited me to go home with her for over Saturday and Sunday. I was very thrilled and also astonished that Mamma allowed me to go.

I enjoyed my visit, but one time did get a little lonesome, which in thinking back does not surprise me, as it was my first experience away from the family. Pearl Rice gave me a beautiful, small glass bowl that held more than a cup of liquid. I forgot that I wasn't home with Mamma while watching its lovely facets reflect light in white, bright blues, oranges, and yellows.

The Rices were Seventh Day Adventists. Their religion was rather hard for me to understand as their time of worship began at sunset on Friday evening and lasted until sunset on Saturday. We were very, very good and quiet on Saturday, so Sunday became the day for fun that weekend.

Mr. Rice took us to school on Monday morning and I really was very happy to see Mamma and Olive.

The following Christmas when Mamma cooked cranberries, she filled my beautiful bowl with the dark red fruit for she said that we children could have our own table.

Olive and I always got so hungry when we had a big company dinner because sometimes we had to eat at the third sitting.

We took six apple boxes and turned them upside down to make a table and covered them with a white tablecloth. We sat on the floor on cushions.

We had everything to eat that big folks had. It was so much fun. Olive and I were joined by Violet and James, Ruth and Elbert Williams (homesteader neighbor's children.)

All of us were very careful to eat properly and be polite. We wanted to make sure we could have our own table in future times. (I still have the beautiful bowl that Pearl Rice gave me.)

CRANBERRIES FOR DINNER

Mamma cooked the cranberries until they were a deep red preserve. She looked over and washed **4 cups of cranberries,** and **added 2 cups of water.** She cooked them until tender and berries quit popping and spewing.

Mamma measured the cooked fruit and added an **equal amount of sugar.** The kettle was pulled to the back of the stove and the berries simmered until the juice was very thick like a preserve. This made a very tasty dessert or a zesty relish for meat. My family today, cleans out a bowl of cranberries cooked in this manner very quickly. They also like the molded cranberry salad as I make it today.

Today, I cook **4 cups cranberries** with **2 cups water** and **2 cups sugar** until the berries quit popping and are tender. Then I pour **3 packages of gelatin,** which has been soaking **in a cup of cold water,** into the hot berries and mix well. Pour into a bowl or mold. When the gelatin sets, unmold onto a serving plate. Cranberries served in this manner are mild and tasty and add a lovely color to the table.

AMBROSIA

We always had ambrosia as one of the traditional desserts for our Christmas or at the home of a relative. Ambrosia may be called "food for the gods," but people also find it very desirable. I even remember ambrosia from my early childhood.

You will need **6 or 8 large sweet oranges, two 15½ oz cans** of either **chunk or sliced unsweetened pineapple, or two pounds of fresh thinly sliced pineapple, 1 pound of fresh coconut,** and about a **cup of sugar.** This amount of sugar varies with the sweetness of the oranges. This will generously serve 12 or more people.

Mamma peeled the oranges the day before Christmas, and we sometimes helped. Every bit of white must come off the orange, because if any were left it made the fruit bitter. Taking off the white peelings was a very tedious job and we got out of it if we could.

Christmas Eve day, Mamma took the good dishes from the top shelves of the kitchen corner cupboard, and carefully washed and dried them. The big glass boat-shaped dish with sparkling facets always was the ambrosia bowl.

On Christmas morning, Mamma made the ambrosia. She quartered the orange with a sharp knife, cutting from top to bottom. She then cut the quarters into thin slices and placed them about 3/4 inches deep in the bottom of the ambrosia bowl. Over the oranges, she put a light sprinkling of sugar, followed by a heavy sprinkling of coconut and oranges again. She kept building, until the bowl was full. It was beautiful to see.

Mamma served the ambrosia individually in small, boat-shaped dishes, that matched the big bowl, generally with whipped cream, ice cream, or snow cream (see below) as a topping. A festive touch is to top the topping with a Maraschino cherry.

When we were able to get canned pineapple, a layer of pineapple alternated with a layer of orange. Eventually, fresh coconuts were shipped into our small markets at Medicine Lake. Mamma thought fresh coconut was much superior to the packaged coconut. A hole was poked in the soft eye of the big nut and the coconut milk was drained into a glass. We each had a little milk to drink.

Ambrosia is a refreshing, colorful dessert and a delightful finish to a big dinner.

SNOW CREAM

We only had snow cream in the coldest of weather, when the mercury dipped far below zero. The snow would fall in feathery softness and accumulate in great piles of pure white, dry snow — no dust, no soot, no pollution.

Mamma whipped up a big bowl of cream until it stood in peaks and added sugar and extract. She folded the feathery snow into the whipped cream and until the cream could absorb no more. That was snow cream! A fluffy white mound of creamy, frosty goodness!

WE HAD TAFFY PULLS

Mamma made a most delicious taffy, so Olive and I learned to both cook and pull taffy at an early age.

Uncle John was also an excellent taffy maker and whenever he came to visit, he was Chief Taffy Cook. Uncle John enjoyed taffy and popcorn so much that Mamma would often say if we were making taffy, "Johnny smells the taffy so much, he will be here." Oddly enough, sometimes he did show up.

The best taffy was made from "soft A" sugar ordered from Sears, Roebuck Grocery Department in Chicago. I have never found this particular grade of sugar in any grocery store.

"Soft A" sugar has the texture of a very good grade brown sugar, with finer grains, and was a very pale cream color. If the taffy was made correctly and pulled long enough, it would cream after standing overnight, and sometimes even in a much shorter time. Creamed taffy is easily crushed into a satiny powder between the fingers and dissolves smoothly in the mouth. Its texture is as soft as ice cream.

SOFT "A" TAFFY

Put **2½ cups "Soft A" sugar** into a **four quart kettle**, stir in **3/4 cup hot water** and **1 tablespoon apple cider vinegar.** Bring to a boil over medium high heat. Be sure the sides of the kettle are cleaned with a damp cloth or paper towel so there are no granules on the sides of the kettle. Important: When the candy starts boiling, do not stir. The kettle must not be moved or jarred.

While the taffy is cooking, **butter a large pan.** When candy is almost at the hard ball stage, add **1 tablespoon of butter.** Test for doneness by dropping a very small amount of syrup into a cup of cold water. Work the test candy around with your fingers. It must be hard, but not brittle. Pour into the well-buttered pan and allow to cool sufficiently to handle. I keep turning the edges to the middle with my fingers as the syrup cools to keep it from becoming too hard to pull. Wash your hands in cold water and dry them thoroughly for pulling the taffy.

Before beginning to pull, poke a hole in the candy with your fingers and put in a teaspoon of your favorite extract. Fold the outside edges over the extract.

Pick up the taffy and begin pulling as soon as you can feasibly handle it and not burn your hands. Hold the taffy as lightly as possible without dropping it as you pull. This allows air holes to form and the finished candy will have a honeycomb appearance, when cut into pieces. Stretch the candy as far as possible as you pull and then double the ends together and continue pulling, repeating the folding operation. If you want to use a triple fold and can manage it, that works all right, too. As you pull the candy, it will soon lose its transparency, turning a light or whitish color.

It is fun for two people to pull on the same candy. They are able to pull it out farther, and they alternate turns in folding back. With a little practice, one person or partners may become quite adept at pulling taffy. If your hands become sticky, either hand the taffy to somebody else to continue pulling or put it back on the buttered pan, quickly wash your hands in *cold* water, thoroughly dry them and you are all ready to continue pulling.

The temptation is great, but don't eat too many samples as you go along. I have never had a stomach upset when I made taffy, but if there are too many tastes, there's not very much left.

Keep stretching out the taffy at the ends as the ends have a tendency to become bulky. When the candy reaches the stage where it becomes almost too stiff to pull, stretch it out into a long rope and place on a large greased pan. Let it set for a few minutes, then press a sharp knife down nearly 2/3 through the taffy. Let set a little longer, turn over and whack with the back of the knife on the back of the taffy opposite the creased line. The taffy will break easily.

TAFFY – NOW

If you followed directions carefully, you will have good taffy. If we could get "Soft A" sugar now, the taffy would almost be sure to cream. Since I am unable to get "Soft A" sugar, I mix **1½ cups of white sugar with 1 cup well-packed light brown sugar, add 3/4 cups of hot water, 2 tablespoons of apple cider vinegar, and 1 tablespoon of butter** and cook to hard ball stage.

The increased amount of vinegar helps to prevent sugaring. This makes good taffy which sometimes creams. The flavor may be rather strong though because of the brown sugar, so get the best quality possible.

A few times, I have had the experience of having my taffy sugar. If it does sugar, recook, add 3/4 cup of water to dissolve it over low heat, add 3 tablespoons vinegar, and cook according to directions. You will be able to taste the vinegar, but the taste combination of vinegar and brown sugar is good.

The quality of the vinegar is not always the same. In fact, I have found a few times that the vinegar did not work, and after changing to another bottle of vinegar, I made excellent taffy.

If you are not particularly interested in your taffy creaming, and want to make doubly sure it won't sugar, add another tablespoon or two of vinegar. Taffy may be made with all white sugar and 4 tablespoons vinegar. It is good, but it will not cream.

Taffy is fun to make, and also delicious to eat, so try it sometime!

TAFFY PULLS AT SCHOOL

On some special Friday afternoons in our prairie school, Mamma allowed the pupils to bring sugar and we had a taffy pull for a treat. Mamma cooked the candy in big kettles over coal-oil stoves.

Imagine the excitement and fun of 20 or 30 young people pulling taffy at one time. Everybody's taffy turned out seemingly well, although I will admit that some had a grimy color. Of course, some ate too much and had very little to take home. At other times, following a program, the community members enjoyed making and pulling candy.

POP CORN

We nearly always popped corn when we made taffy. Corn poppers make easy chore of popping corn, but we popped corn in our big iron skillet or big iron pot. Heat the container until it is quite hot, add **2 tablespoons lard**, a **teaspoon salt**. When lard is melted, pour in **5 or 6 handsfull of popcorn**, stir with a long handled spoon until the first grains begin to pop, quickly put the cover on and shake or push the container until the corn is popped. The movement keeps the corn from burning.

The corn is now ready to eat. If you like, you may dribble some melted butter over the popcorn, but the lard gives it a good flavor, and I hardly ever use the melted butter.

Two or three big pieces of chewy taffy, a bowl of hot popcorn, and a good book made many happy cozy evenings in rainy or cold weather.

POPCORN BALLS

Sometimes Mamma did not make taffy, but made popcorn balls. By shaking the container of popped corn, the hard or unpopped grains would settle to the bottom. Then she removed the popped corn to a 8 or 10 quart dish pan or mixing bowl.

Six quarts of popped corn will make 14 to 15 popcorn balls the size of an orange.

Following is a recipe for the popcorn syrup. Stir together **2 cups brown sugar, 2 tablespoons vinegar,** and **½ cup water.** Bring to boil and cook until a hard ball is formed in cold water. Just before it reaches the hard ball stage add **1 tablespoon of butter.** Pour over the popcorn and mix well with a big spoon.

As soon as you are able to handle the corn without burning your hands, start forming the balls, Press the corn lightly into balls, being careful not to crush the corn.

I think we relished these popcorn balls more, because Mamma usually made them on a stormy day, when we couldn't go outdoors.

SORGHUM CANDY

Sorghum candy and sorghum taffy are both very good. For sorghum candy, use **1½ cups white sugar** and **1 cup sorghum or molasses, ½ cup water** and **3 tablespoons vinegar, 1 tablespoon butter** and cook to a firm but not quite hard ball stage. Always remember not to stir the candy or jar the kettle while cooking. As you take the candy from the stove, stir in a **teaspoon of soda** and add a **cup or two of black walnuts.** Pour into a **large, well-buttered cooky pan.** When cold, cut into one inch squares, and wrap each square in waxed paper, twisting the ends, like candy kisses.

SORGHUM TAFFY

Sorghum taffy is made by using the same proportions as used for the sorghum and black walnut candy, but omit the walnuts and soda. When the syrup makes a hard ball in cold water, pour it into a greased pan and allow to cool for pulling. This makes a very tasty taffy, but it will not cream. It may also be wrapped in wax paper. It will keep for weeks and still be delicious.

WHERE THE SORGHUM CORN GROWS

Sorghum is excellent in any recipe that calls for molasses, but it is sometimes difficult to obtain a good quality sorghum. One summer after I was grown, Mamma and I drove to Indiana. Sorghum was scarce that year, but Mamma was determined to have some sorghum. One morning, we drove for several miles down on the flats by the Ohio river. Whenever we saw a sign with sorghum, (even if the sign was old) we would stop. But they said, "Had a poor crop this year. We aren't selling any sorghum." Mamma was getting discouraged, but we kept going. Finally we stopped at a place of an older man. As we talked and the man found out that Mamma was one of the Romines, he loosened up and sold us 2 gallons of sorghum. He had hunted fox with Uncle Sid and Uncle Bert.

I can still almost hear the deep, doleful baying of the fox hounds as they followed a fox trail through the woods. It was a terribly mournful sound, and when I was small, if I were awakened in the night, the lonesomeness left me feeling very alone and frightened.

Sorghum corn grows well in a moist, warm climate. The stalks are cut before the leaves start drying, then deleafed, cleaned and crushed. They then go through a press and the juice is caught and boiled down until it becomes thick and is then "sorghum molasses."

Mamma had read us stories about making maple sugar in Vermont. When they had "sugaring off" the children took pans of snow and poured spoonsful of the thick, hot maple syrup on the snow. This would harden the syrup into chewy portions of maple syrup. It certainly seemed to be a wonderful thing to do. Once Mamma made a large batch of sorghum taffy and we got pans of hard snow and dipped some of the syrup over the snow. It quickly hardened and was delightfully chewy. I am sure this was every bit as good, if not better, than the maple syrup enjoyed by the children of Vermont.

ALTITUDE CHANGES

Variance in altitudes from sea-level to mountain areas above 3000 feet may make it necessary to make some adjustments in temperature in cooking and amount of liquid, sugar, and shortening used.

The higher the altitude, the lower the air pressure, so water boils sooner at a lower pressure. This difference in boiling points affects the cooking time of vegetables, eggs, candies, and the texture of baked foods.

Many times people move to an area with a big altitude change and discover that their favorite cake recipe is not satisfactory. This situation can be corrected by making altitude adjustments.

At sea level the boiling point of water is 212.0°F and at 5000 feet it is 202.6°F, as a simple illustration of the difference.

In most cook books, the recipes are written for lower altitudes, and need little adjustment until after 3000 feet, but since my home altitude is 5000 feet, I make adjustments for cakes.

Quick breads, biscuits and muffins need very little change. A yeast bread may rise too quickly at the higher altitude, so work and knead down three times instead of two before putting loaves in the pans for baking.

Decrease the amount of baking powder or soda (leavening) approximately one-half at 5000 feet. Increase baking temperature 3°F for each 1000 feet. Here in the mountains, I use an increase of 25°. Add 2 extra tablespoons flour for each cup of flour used. It may be necessary to use 3 extra tablespoons liquid per cup.

None of these adjustments are absolute, as the amounts are different in different recipes. It is better to make just one adjustment at a time. To get the best results, it is necessary to work with the recipe until you know the best combination for your recipe and altitude.

At the higher altitudes, it is necessary to boil foods longer than at sea level to obtain the same results. For instance, a 3 minute egg at sea level might be a 5 minute egg at 5000 feet.

The following recipe, Aunt Emma's Regulation Butter Cake, is evidently written for a much lower altitude than the 5000 feet at which I live. Aunt Emma lived at less than 3000 feet. This is the original recipe.

AUNT EMMA'S BUTTER CAKE

Cream ½ **cup butter** and gradually add **1 cup of sugar** and beat until fluffy. Add **2 cups of sifted cake flour** and 2/3 **cups milk** to the butter and sugar. Add just about a fourth of the flour and liquid at a time — beat well after each addition. Add **4 teaspoons baking powder** and **1 teaspoon vanilla extract.** Fold in the **3 egg whites** that have been stiffly beaten. Bake in **two 8" cake pans** for 30 minutes at medium heat, 350°.

This is the original recipe and I followed these proportions carefully. The cake had a very good taste, but the texture was coarse.

I used the same recipe, but made the altitude adjustments for 5000 feet. I used **2 cups + 2 tablespoons sifted cake flour,** 2/3 **cup + 2 tablespoons milk** and used only **2 teaspoons baking powder.** I baked the cake at 375° for 30 minutes.

I had an excellent cake with a fine, fluffy texture. I baked this cake 3 times making one adjustment each time. I have used the original recipes as I found them in Mamma's recipes in this book and I have adjusted according to the mountain altitude when I myself bake them.

It would be well for a person to check with the United States Extension Service in your locality if the altitude where you live varies, so you will have accurate and detailed information as to changes. Also, remember that the proportions in the cake recipes may vary, so no set adjustment may be given for all cakes. The adjustments are relevant.

MOST COOKBOOKS ARE WRITTEN FOR THE LOWER ALTITUDES — that is sea level up to 2000 to 3000 feet.

OLIVE BAKES A CAKE

Not long after I learned to make buttermilk biscuits, I learned to bake a plain white cake. This helped Mamma, because then she did not have to bother with making a dessert for our school lunch boxes.

One day Olive wanted very badly to make a cake. Mamma was busy, so she told me to help. Olive had found a recipe for a white cake on the side of a coconut box that she wanted to try. Since it was her first cake, I told her to make just half a recipe so she wouldn't waste material.

So Olive made the cake that was to become a family tradition. She couldn't read all the directions, but I helped her figure out the words. She was very serious about doing everything just right. That cake was baked in an old-fashioned drum oven.

A drum oven is of a light weight double wall tin material, with approximately 2 inches space between the walls and placed between sections of stove pipe about 12 to 16 inches above the stove. It is heated by the hot air from the stove passing between the double walls. Our oven was around 18 inches long and 10 inches wide, inside measurements. A damper in the pipe above the oven controlled the heat in the oven. When the damper was closed or partially closed, it prevented the heat from going up in the pipe.

The heat in the oven was tested by sticking a hand in the open oven.

Some homesteaders had upstair rooms or attics. The stove pipe would run up through these rooms and they used these drum ovens as a method of heating.

Olive's cake came from the oven a light toasty brown, tender and flaky. My little sister had made the perfect cake. Everybody praised her and praised the cake, and just couldn't understand why I didn't have her make the entire recipe. I didn't either. Mamma liked that recipe so much that she used it when she wanted a particularly festive cake. The original cake had three eggs, but Mamma substituted the whites of five or six (depending on the size of the egg) and made a superb two layer white cake. (There was also enough batter to make *six cupcakes.*)

COCONUT CAKE

Thoroughly cream **2 cups sugar** and **½ cup butter** until very light and fluffy. Use **1 cup of milk** and **3 cups of sifted cake flour.** Add ¼ of the milk and ¼ of the flour at a time and beat thoroughly each time until all the milk and flour are used. Stir in **2 teaspoons baking powder.** Beat the whites of the eggs until they stand in stiff peaks. Fold the whites into the cake batter and beat by hand 200 times. The electric beater may be used, but the texture is not the same, and the hand method really seems to be superior as the cake is more moist. Just before pouring into pans, flavor with **1 teaspoon vanilla,** and fold in **stiffly beaten egg whites.**

Divide the cake batter evenly into two 9" round cake pans, and lightly spread from the center to the sides, so there is a slight 5 inch wide depression in the center of the dough. This will help to keep the layers flat, for a cake has a tendency to raise in the center while cooking.

Bake for 25 minutes in a 375° preheated oven. Test for doneness by inserting a toothpick into the cake, and if it comes out clean the cake is done. Another way to test is to very lightly touch the top of the cake with your finger and if the surface comes quickly back into place, the cake is done. (Adjust recipe for altitudes over 3000 feet. See page 150)

When baked, place the cake on a rack and cool in the pans. When cool, remove the cakes from the pans. Have a large flat cake plate ready and put a layer on the plate, top side down. Spread on filling or frosting. Next place the second layer with the bottom down. If the top of this layer is not level, take a long, thin, very sharp knife and carefully cut the top off, then use filling or frosting.

Completely frost the entire cake.

Mamma used ground fresh coconut in the filling and in the frosting if she could get it, otherwise, she used the packaged coconut.

POWDERED SUGAR FROSTING

Mamma used a powdered sugar frosting at first. She took **2 cups powdered sugar, 4 tablespoons of butter** which was thoroughly worked into the sugar, then she slowly added either **hot milk** or **hot water** 1 teaspoon at a time, working it into the sugar and butter. She was very careful to get just enough liquid to make the sugar beatable and beat it until it was fluffy, then added **extract.**

If you are generous in your use of frosting, it may be necessary to use **3 cups of powdered sugar** and **6 tablespoons butter.** It will, of course, need **more hot water** or **hot milk.** After you frost each layer, sprinkle generously with ground coconut.

Sometimes Mamma used a boiled frosting that was similar to divinity, in that the hot syrup was poured over the stiffly beaten white of an egg. The next frosting used was a seven minute frosting and I think these proportions are very satisfactory.

SEVEN MINUTE FROSTING

Put **1½ cups sugar, whites of 2 large eggs** or **3 small eggs, 1 table-spoon white corn syrup** or **white Karo, 1/3 cup water,** and **1/8 teaspoon of salt in the top of a double boiler** and mix two minutes. Have the water boiling in the bottom part of a double boiler, place the top over the boiling water and continue beating for seven minutes. I use my electric hand mixer. The frosting must stand in stiff peaks. When done, add **1 teaspoon of your favorite extract,** remove from heat and beat one minute more.

Mix **1½ cups of this frosting** with **1 cup of fresh ground coconut.** This is enough filling for the two layers. Frost the top layer and sides of the cake, with the remainder and sprinkle the top generously with the fresh coconut and if sprinkling is not sufficient for the sides, lightly pat on more coconut by hand.

ELSIE'S CHOCOLATE CAKE

I had told my grandson, Michael, I would bake him a cake for his fifth birthday, and when he asked for a chocolate cake instead of the usual angel food, I took out Elsie's chocolate cake recipe.

Cream **2 cups sugar** and **½ cup butter.** Add the beaten **yolks of 2 eggs** and beat well. Beat the **whites of the 2 eggs** until they form very stiff peaks and set aside. Dissolve **1 scant tablespoon soda** in **¼ cup boiling water** and mix well with the sugar, butter and egg yolks until well creamed. Dissolve **2 heaping tablespoons unsweetened cocoa** in **3/4 cup hot water** and add to the prepared mixture.

Add **2½ cups sifted flour** with **1 cup sour milk** alternating flour and milk and beat well each time until the mixture is light and fluffy. Now gently fold in the stiffly beaten egg whites until no white shows. Spoon the batter evenly into **three 9" cake pans** and place in a 350° preheated oven. Cook for 30 minutes or until done when a toothpick inserted comes out clean. When done, set pans on a rack or bread board to cool.

While waiting for the cake to cool, make a powdered sugar chocolate frosting.

POWDERED SUGAR CHOCOLATE FROSTING

Mix **3 rounded tablespoons cocoa** with **3 cups of powdered sugar.** Work **6 tablespoons butter** thoroughly into the sugar and cocoa. It will probably take **6 tablespoons of boiling water or hot coffee,** but first just add 3 tablespoons of the hot liquid, then mix. Add liquid just one teaspoonful at a time until the frosting has the consistency of a thick cake batter. Put in **1 teaspoon of vanilla** and beat until light and creamy.

Place the first layer of the cake top down, on a large plate. Spread a scant ¼ of the frosting evenly on this layer. Place the second layer bottom down on the frosted layer. If the second layer is not level on top, cut even by slicing off top with a very sharp slender knife. Spread a scant ¼ of the frosting on this layer and add the third layer bottom down.

You have slightly more than half of the frosting left, so frost the top layer and spread over the sides. You may give the cake a decorative effect by swirling the frosting with a knife dipped in hot water (then shake off the water). This may be done on the sides, too.

If you want only a two layer cake, keep one layer refrigerated for a day or two. Make a hot sauce and pour over the refrigerated cake and serve to your Garden Club.

CHOCOLATE SAUCE

I like a chocolate sauce. Thoroughly mix **1 cup sugar** and **1 heaping tablespoon cocoa** with **4 tablespoons flour** in the **top of a double boiler.** Pour in **1 cup boiling water** while stirring constantly, add **4 tablespoons butter.** Cook for 15 to 20 minutes stirring every few minutes. Add **1 teaspoon vanilla extract.** This sauce is quite thick and is excellent served either hot or cold over bread, unfrosted cake, or puddings.

— When baking this cake, adjust measurements if you live at a higher altitude. It is really an excellent cake.

AUNT HATTIE'S ONE EGG CHOCOLATE CAKE

When Mamma and the various aunts or older cousins got together, they always exchanged recipes. I am especially fond of chocolate cake, and this cake from Aunt Hattie's collection is very good.

Bring **1 cup of water** to a boil in a small kettle and add **1 square of bitter chocolate.** As soon as the chocolate melts, cool the liquid.

Cream ¼ **cup butter** with **1 cup of sugar. Add 1 egg yolk** well beaten. Then stir in the chocolate mixture. Sift and gradually add 1¾ **cups flour** beating well after each addition. **Fold in 2 teaspoons baking powder, 1 teaspoon vanilla** and the **one stiffly beaten egg white.** Bake in a (350°) moderate oven in a 8" x 12" **loaf pan** for 25 minutes or until a toothpick comes clean when inserted in the center of the cake.

Make a chocolate frosting with powdered sugar.

Most of these cakes need adjustments for higher altitudes.

HOME REMEDIES

To the settlers on the prairies, home remedies were essential to their way of life — and in some cases, saved lives. A sick or injured person could be hauled many miles in a buggy or rough jolting wagon to a doctor where the same treatment might be continued with a palliative or a pain killer added.

Hot water with salt or salts could pull out infection from a disease-infected wound and perhaps prevent blood poisoning. (Either place the wound directly into the water, or put hot packs on the troublesome spot.) Boric acid dissolved in hot water was used, also.

Salt pork or bacon placed immediately over an infected sore might bring the infection to a head so it could be lanced to relieve the pan and possibly prevent more infection.

Each household had its own type of medication and the following are some methods used by my family.

(I am not recommending these, only giving what was *used.*)

WHITE LINIMENT

On the homestead, it was not always convenient to go 35 miles to Culbertson or 10 miles to Flandrem and later Medicine Lake (9 miles) for supplies. (Flandrem was moved to the railroad when it came through, and the name was changed to Medicine Lake.)

Grandpa kept a supply of home remedies on hand. One of these remedies was "white liniment." The proportions are as follows: (Remember, the prices are those quoted in the early 1900's. I checked with the druggist and he said the price would now be approximately five times more.)

Hartshorne, 3 ounces; arnica, 2 ounces; witchhazel, 2 ounces; camphor gum, 5¢; 3 eggs; and 1 pint apple cider vinegar.

Beat the eggs several strokes with a fork, and put all ingredients into a quart fruit jar and shake well.

This liniment was used on animals as well as people for aches, bruises, sprains, or muscle pains.

It developed a strong odor and was always kept on hand. It did relieve pain — whether, the odor, the idea of medication, or the actual ingredients were responsible, I do not know.

ECZEMA

A small cousin had eczema and this recipe was used.

Use **$.25 worth of hydrate of chloral** and **$.10 of camphor gum.** Stir together equal parts until a liquid is formed. Mix this liquid with enough **vaseline** to make an ointment. Rub on two or three times a day.

YELLOW ROOT AND POTASH

Yellow root and potash was a mixture that Mamma used when I had a sore throat. I do not know how it was made, but it was a deep yellow liquid. Mamma would wrap a clean white rag around her finger, dip it in the solution and wash out my throat. It was a horrible concoction, but my throat did get better.

The following story was pieced together from things overheard and absorbed, for it was a "hush, hush matter."

A neighbor's boy had a very bad sore throat, and it seems it was diphtheria or they thought it was diphtheria. Mamma would go and wash out that child's throat three times a day. She then changed her clothes and washed very thoroughly. If she used a disinfectant, I don't know what it was, but neither Olive nor I got a sore throat. The neighbors credited the Doctor and Mamma with saving the life of their little boy.

HAND LOTION

The following items do make an excellent hand lotion. Soak **20 grams gum tragacanth in 19 ounces of rose water** for two days. Mix well and add **1 ounce glycerine** and **1 ounce of alcohol.** This much hand lotion lasts several weeks and does keep the hands smooth and soft.

Mamma was very particular about the care of her hands. She always wore gloves and her hands were soft and white. Her finger nails were clean and neatly trimmed.

GOOSE GREASE AND TURPENTINE

One-half cup goose grease and **1 tablespoon turpentine** were well mixed and used as a remedy for sore throat and colds. Mix the ingredients thoroughly, heat and rub on to the throat, chest and back. Cover the greased areas with a heated piece of woolen underwear or part of an old woolen blanket. Wrap with a towel to keep the heat in. I hated this, but it must have worked — I lived!

If goose grease wasn't available, lard was substituted.

Note: — A person's own dirty stocking with the foot next to the flesh was supposed to cure sore throats!

MUSTARD PLASTER

Mustard plasters were used to break congestion in the chest. Use a proportion of **4 tablespoons of dry mustard** and **6 tablespoons of flour.** Add enough **cold water** to make a thick paste. Spread this paste on two pieces of muslin large enough to cover the lung area, back and front. Wrap the patient in sheets. Leave plaster on for 20 minutes.

The unlucky victim usually ends up with very red or blistered skin from the mustard whether the remedy served its purpose or not.

ONION POULTICE

A strong and very odorous poultice was made from fried onions. Use a **large skillet, add ½ cup lard** and melt. Fill the skillet with **sliced onions** and cook until mushy. Allow to cool until the onions may be touched with the bare hand.

Make two poultices — one for the back and one for the chest — by placing the fried onions between two layers of cloth. Cover the affected areas with the poultices, and spread a heavy blanket over the patient. The cooked onion smell lingers for weeks. Some people literally swear by the poultice — others swear at it.

BROWN PAPER FOR CUTS

Grandpa wrapped strips of a brown paper sack around a cut and bleeding finger. He pulled the edges of the wound together, then the paper was put on and fastened. The blood soaked the paper, dried and caked. He left the brown paper on for a few days, and the cut always seemed to heal without any difficulty.

FLAX SEED IN THE EYES

A flax seed was used if any object got into the eyes. Just place a flax seed in the eye, and it would "chase" the dirt out by morning.

DIARRHEA

Treatments:

1. Make a thick paste of **2 tablespoons flour** and **2 tablespoons water** and swallow as quickly as possible to keep from gagging.

2. Boil a **cup of milk,** add enough **thickener** to make quite stiff, season with a **pinch of salt,** and a **teaspoon of black pepper.** Use more pepper if you are able to stand it.

3. Drink **hot black coffee** with a generous amount of **black pepper.**

4. Drink **hot black tea** with a generous amount of **black pepper.**

GREASE TO TAKE OUT GREASE

Axle grease may be removed from clothing by thoroughly rubbing with a generous amount of bacon grease or lard. After the axle grease is loosened, rub soap on the spot, then wash out in warm water. (This works.)

THE END OF FEASTING

I think Mamma must have believed in preventative medicine. At least she practiced it in matters of catharics.

When we had an extra good dinner with many sweets and rich foods, Olive and I had to take a physic, whether we *needed* it or not. I remember castoria — it was effective and I rather liked the taste. It was the same with Syrup of Figs — that wasn't bad either. Then some neighbor gave Mamma a recipe for a home-made catharic. The taste was terrible, I thought, but it certainly was most effective — and many a

trip was made to the little house out back — even though the thermometer registered below zero.

Grind ½ pound seeded raisins, ½ pound figs, and 1 ounce of senna leaves. Add 1 pound of brown sugar. Pour over this mixture ½ pint of boiling water. Stir thoroughly. One *dose* was one generous teaspoon of this concoction.

As I have already remarked, it was effective.

MAKING LAUNDRY SOAP

Mamma made laundry soap and used the fats left over from beef and hog butchering.

I remember when Grandma made soap back in Indiana. Quantities of wood ashes had been saved, and Grandpa made lye by pouring water through the ashes which drained into containers. He built a fire under the great iron pot which was hanging from a tripod outdoors. Then he put several pounds of fat into the pot and poured the wood lye over it. That was once my inquisitiveness was nipped in the bud very promptly. I had to stand back and watch Grandma stir the fat and lye with a big wooden spoon. I never did see what was happening in that kettle.

It seemed a very long time that Grandma stirred and stirred. Grandpa came occasionally and put more wood under the kettle so the fire continued to burn and the soap mixture to bubble.

Finally, Grandma decided the soap had cooked enough and Grandpa ladled it out into flat pans or wooden boxes. When it began to harden, Grandpa took a big knife and cut it into bars. It was allowed to stand for two or three days, before he took it from the boxes and broke the bars apart. The soap bars dried for two or three weeks before it was stored — and there was a year's supply of laundry soap.

Soap is easy to make, but a word of precaution — wear rubber gloves, and if you have one, a rubber apron.

The following recipe will make an excellent household soap. Use 6 cups of rendered fat (either lard or tallow), and ½ of a 13 oz. can of lye. You may purchase the lye at most grocery stores. Melt the fat slowly over low heat in a six quart stainless steel or enamel kettle until it is only slightly warm when touched with a finger.

Dissolve the lye in 2½ cups of soft water in a one quart enamel or glass container. Pour very slowly into the melted fat. When the lye is dissolved in the water, the liquid becomes very hot; in fact, it boils. Allow it to cool, then pour it gradually into the fat, meanwhile stirring slowly with a wooden spoon. Keep stirring for almost half an hour or until the mixture has the consistency of cream. Pour this soft soap into flat boxes that have been lined with waxed paper. Allow to stand for 24 hours, remove from box and cut into bars. Age for two or three weeks.

I like homemade soap for laundry as it is an excellent cleaning agent. Scrape flakes from the bar of soap and dissolve in hot water, before adding to the washing machine.

I must emphasize that a person be extremely careful in handling the lye, as it can be very dangerous. Use rubber gloves and if you have one, a rubber apron. Have enamel, stainless steel, or glass containers for the lye. If any lye gets on exposed surface of body, wash immediately and thoroughly in water. Vinegar also is an excellent neutralizer for lye.

Some suggestions: — If the mixture does not thicken within 20 to 30 minutes, it may be too warm. Cool by running cold water into the sink and setting the kettle into the water. Continue the slow stirring.

If the soap mixture is lumpy when it sets, add 5 cups of water. Dissolve over low heat, then cook until it thickens. Pour in molds.

GRANDPA GOES HOME TO INDIANA

When the family claims were filed on in the fall of 1906, the land was wide-open prairie. Grandpa surveyed the land, and when the government surveyors came in the spring of 1907, they found that he was only a foot or two off.

At first the homesteaders were only allowed to file on 160 acres and it took 5 years to "prove-up," or to obtain the deed to the land. That law was soon changed to 320 acres. At that time, Mamma relinquished her claim north of Grandpa, so he could file on her original claim and she filed on 320 acres about 3½ miles northeast.

The homesteader had to live on his claim a certain specified time, build a house and do plowing and fencing.

Grandpa's homestead home was headquarters for the gathering of the family and sometimes in the summers, all the sons and daughters and even nieces and nephews and their children arrived. Great amounts of food were cooked and consumed, and there was much talking and laughing among the adults and much noise as the children played hide and seek, croquet, and jumped rope.

But sometimes when the confusion became too great, Grandpa took his hoe and went to the garden. There he worked and when tiring, we could see him leaning on his hoe handle, gazing into the distances of that great land. I wondered at times if he was thinking of Grandma.

Grandpa lived long enough to "prove-up" on his claim and died at the age of 79 on Christmas Eve in 1912.

Uncle John took Grandpa back to Indiana. Many friends and relatives met the train and attended the funeral. Grandpa was buried beside Grandma in the family graveyard back of Old Pigeon Church where his family and the families of his forebearers had worshipped for so many years.

Many more stories could be told — many more recipes could be written, but — this book is finished.

I have enjoyed the kitchen-testing and I have so enjoyed the many additional guests that have come to our home to eat the many foods that I have cooked.

I have taken many memory journeys back to my childhood, and have developed a longing to return to the prairies where I might gaze across the great distances, watch a brilliant, far-flung sunset, see once again the magnificent array of weaving, waving color masses of the northern lights, feel the insidious cold of the first wild blizzard as it assaults the prairies.

If I did return, my joints, that sometimes twinge just a little, would keep me from chasing the agile cottontails. But I can still make a rabbit pie.

It might take an extra hour or two, but I could still scrub the clothes on the old washboard and put them out, brightly clean, to flutter in the wind.

I might lean on the hoe handle occasionally, as Grandpa used to do, just looking across the distant miles to the low hills on the reservation. But I could still hoe the garden and have all those crispy fresh vegetables.

I might not be able to do the schottishe and the polka as nimbly as the fiddler plays the tunes, but I can still do the old fashioned waltz.

Yes, I could still be happy on my far flung prairies — wheat fields now.

INDEX

Editor:
Thomas K. Worcester

Design:
Dean McMullen